THIRTY YEARS BEHIND THE GLASS

30 THIRTY YEARS

BEHIND THE GLASS

From Otis Redding and

Stax Records to

Santana's Supernatural

JIM GAINES
As Told to
LEE ZIMMERMAN

TEXAS A&M UNIVERSITY PRESS
COLLEGE STATION

∞ This paper meets the requirements of ANSI/NISO Z39.48-1992 (Permanence of Paper). Binding materials have been chosen for durability.

Manufactured in the United States of America

LIBRARY OF CONGRESS CATALOGING-IN-PUBLICATION DATA

Names: Zimmerman, Lee, author. | Gaines, Jim.
Title: Thirty years behind the glass : from Otis Redding and Stax Records to Santana's
    Supernatural / Jim Gaines as told to Lee Zimmerman.
Description: First edition. | College Station : Texas A&M University Press, [2022] |
    Includes index.
Identifiers: LCCN 2022015962 | ISBN 9781648431005 (cloth) | ISBN 9781648431012 (ebook)
Subjects: LCSH: Gaines, Jim. | Sound engineers—United States—Biography. |
    Sound recording executives and producers—United States—Biography. |
    Popular music—Production and direction—United States—History—20th century.
Classification: LCC ML429.G135 .Z56 2022 | DDC 781.49/092
    [B]—dc23/eng/20220405
LC record available at https://lccn.loc.gov/2022015962

UNLESS OTHERWISE INDICATED, ALL PHOTOGRAPHS
ARE FROM JIM GAINES'S PERSONAL COLLECTION.

To my wife, Sandy Carroll Gaines, for her support,

and to my daughters, Karen Dantzler and Connie Johnson.

—Jim Gaines

I dedicate this book to my wife, Alisa Cherry,

for her constant love and support,

and to my sons, Chris and Kyle, for being who they are.

—Lee Zimmerman

CONTENTS

A gallery of photographs follows page 96.

ACKNOWLEDGMENTS

Big thanks to Lee Zimmerman for all the hard work and making this trip a reality. To all the staff at Texas A&M University Press for their great work, and for believing in me and my story. To Bob Taylor for our friendship and his great eye from behind the camera. To Laurel Anderton, a fantastic and patient copyeditor. To all the artists, crews, studios, and colorful characters that made these stories come to life. To Jody Stevens and Jeff Powell for taking the time to sort through photos. To everyone who contributed to my life journey in the music industry.

—JIM GAINES

Special thanks to Jim Gaines for allowing me to share his remarkable story.

—LEE ZIMMERMAN

THIRTY YEARS BEHIND THE GLASS

CHAPTER 1

Memphis Is Burning!

APRIL 4, 1968

IT WAS 6:00 P.M. on what had been an average day, but Jim Gaines suddenly realized that nothing was going to be normal from this point forward. He had left the studio where he worked to grab a quick hamburger, and as he was driving back to continue working on the jingles he was scheduled to record that evening, he realized that his surroundings had taken on an unfamiliar, menacing appearance. To Gaines, it seemed almost as if he were driving toward a war zone.

Smoke hovered over the Memphis skyline. Sirens wailed, the sound ripping through the usual quiet of the falling dusk. Gaines remembers being quickly filled with dread and anxiety. What was going on?

Memphis was burning.

Gaines remembers switching on WDIA radio, the leading Memphis soul station and his preferred music source. The deejay's voice, coming through the speakers in his car, sounded unsteady. He reported that Martin Luther King Jr. had been shot.

Dr. King had been in Memphis to intercede in a strike by local sanitation workers. The civil rights leader had hoped to bring a voice of reason to the conflict and calm the situation so that negotiations could continue toward gaining the city's underpaid employees the compensation they deserved.

Gaines heard the words coming from his radio, but somehow the news still didn't seem real. The night before, according to earlier reports, Dr. King had told a gathering of people that he had "been to the mountaintop" and assured his hearers that one day they would reach the envisioned "Promised Land." King had even hinted, in that fateful speech, that he might not live long enough to make the journey with his listeners. To Gaines, those words now seemed darkly prophetic.

Gaines, a White man born and raised in the South, worked alongside Black musicians and support staff each day. He also worked a part-time job at Stax Records, a company that, like Motown in Detroit, made music designed to appeal to listeners both Black and White. This was rhythm and blues-infused rock and roll, the sound of the 1960s: popular music that was sweeping the nation and the world, especially among young people.

But in this moment it was difficult to think about anything joyful or exciting. Gaines walked back into the studio, realizing that no more recording work would be accomplished on this particular night. The jingle session planned for that evening was quickly canceled. As the musicians showed up, Gaines told them to go home.

From the jingle studio, Gaines called Stax and talked to Ronnie Capone, a man he considered his mentor. Ronnie had worked at the jingle company but had recently taken a full-time position at the Stax record label. Gaines, already working part time there when Capone arrived, had been hired by Steve Cropper, guitarist and de facto director of artists and repertoire for the label, and Jim Stewart, co-owner of the company. Gaines was now eight months into his part-time work at Stax.

"I asked Ronnie how they were doing at Stax," Gaines recalls. "He said they were going to load up as many master tapes as possible in their cars and get them out of the building. He asked if I could come over and load up as many as I could carry."

The studio had received threats in the past from local ruffians who had hinted they would do damage to the building unless they were paid to stay away. The chaotic atmosphere surrounding Dr. King's assassination seemed to provide a perfect opportunity, and it seemed they were now bent on taking advantage. Stax had hired security guards to help protect the place, but Gaines wasn't sure whether they were more than one step above the people making the threats.

Gaines admired Ronnie Capone, thinking him probably the best recording engineer in Memphis, and he was eager to assist. By the time Gaines arrived at the Stax studios, Capone, along with Steve Cropper, had already loaded a number of tapes. Despite the turmoil embroiling the city a few miles away, the process went smoothly, Gaines recalls.

By the time they finished, a nearby shopping center was in flames. Looters were everywhere. Ultimately, though, Stax would be spared. The sign out front was damaged, but the building itself suffered no noticeable harm.

But the effect of these disturbing events on the collective psyche was far more difficult to discern, Gaines would later say. Dr. King had been beloved by the entire Stax organization, and the fact that he had been killed in the city they called home was a cause for deep sorrow. In the days ahead, Memphis would see curfews, additional civic strife, and troops stationed on city streets. Even to this day, for Gaines, the scars have not fully healed.

"The fact that Dr. King, a man intent on binding the wounds, would be shot in my city had a profound effect on me," he insists, more than half a century later. "That terrible memory still haunts me, even now."

In a career spanning five decades, Jim Gaines has seen a lot and experienced a lot more. He has been an eyewitness to the creation of some of the most influential music recordings of the twentieth century. In fact, with consummate skill, he has had a hand in shaping the sound of the twentieth century. Jim Gaines's life in the studio has given him a front-row seat for some of the most important music making in recent history. And it all started in Memphis, the city built on the bluffs above the Mississippi River, when a young man suddenly faced a life-changing decision.

CHAPTER 2

Humble Beginnings

1960–1968

THE MAN WHO WOULD later go on to help create a signature sound for such legendary artists as Steve Miller, Carlos Santana, Huey Lewis and the News, Stevie Ray Vaughan, and other well-known artists had, by his own admission, humble beginnings.

A self-described "hard-working hillbilly from Arkansas," Jim Gaines made his entry into the world of recording in 1960. At that time, Gaines had taken his entrance exams for Memphis State University, but his girlfriend's unexpected pregnancy forced him to put his plans for higher education on the back burner in favor of immediate employment. He had quit a job in the shipping department of a snack food company when he was still planning to go to college. But now he had to get a new gig—and soon.

In 1960, he found himself working as an errand boy for a Memphis advertising company called Pepper-Tanner that specialized in creating radio jingles. Gaines realized that there was something about the atmosphere of the studio where the tracks were recorded that appealed to him. Even though in the beginning he was scarcely within shouting distance of the upper tier of management, he had a sense that this industry was where he wanted to be.

In the eight years he worked at Pepper-Tanner, Gaines quickly moved up the ranks and gained more responsibility as he proved his mettle. "We had two groups of singers working eight hours a day, doing the recordings our clients had ordered," he recalls. "I worked an eight-hour shift, and often I'd be on call other times as well. Basically I was a glorified go-fer, but it didn't matter. I was determined to move up in the company and do whatever I had to do to make it happen."

One way Gaines made a name for himself at Pepper-Tanner was by essentially creating his own areas of responsibility, duplicating tapes and mixing the recordings when other engineers were unavailable. "I told my boss one day that we needed a person to start this new position," Gaines said. "When he asked who that would be, I said, 'Me.' So I started the next week."

Ultimately, Jim Gaines would run Pepper-Tanner's studios in Memphis and oversee the operations of another studio the company owned in Dallas. Through hard work and creativity, he molded himself into a young executive with a decent salary, a company car, and stock in the corporation.

While he was working at Pepper-Tanner, Gaines became acquainted with a pair of studio musicians who often played on night jingle sessions. Their names were Booker T. Jones and Steve Cropper.

"After working with Steve a couple of times," Gaines says, "he asked me after a session one night if I would come over and talk to Jim Stewart at Stax about doing some part-time work for them. I met with Jim and Steve, and they asked if I could work a few nights a week for them, mainly to start a tape library.

"When I went there the first day, they took me to the control room, which used to be the stage of the movie theater that was previously housed in the building," Gaines recalls. "In the corner, there were stacks of boxes that weren't labeled at all. They wanted me to go through everything and start a library by marking the tape boxes and identifying the music they contained. In the process, I got to hear a lot of early recordings. They were mostly four-track and mono [single-track] recordings. But every once in a while, a stereo mix would be made that would be used for an album. Back in those days they were referred to as 'high fidelity.'"

Gaines began splitting his time between Pepper-Tanner and Stax: working his regular shift during the day at the former and spending three to four nights a week at the latter. He would come to look on his time at Stax as his big break.

"Recording was done at a converted movie palace where I used to see movies as a kid," Gaines remembers. "It was called the Capitol Theater. The facility included two studios. The area once occupied by the movie screen was converted into a control room. The technology was simple as well. Only mono and four-tracks were available for recording, and as a result, everything was cut straight to mono most of the time." Stereo recording had been on the market in a limited way since about 1955, but it would be the late 1960s before the stereo format would begin to dominate the music recording industry.

His part-time gig at Stax afforded Gaines the opportunity to meet some of the heavy hitters in the music industry of the day. Steve Cropper was already known as an outstanding guitarist and producer. Booker T. Jones's keyboards provided the essential background to many of the company's iconic recordings. Al Jackson on drums and Donald "Duck" Dunn on bass provided solid backing for many popular recordings. All of these musicians were heavily involved in the songwriting that would eventually materialize as hits by artists like the Bar-Kays, Rufus Thomas, Sam and Dave, Albert King, Little Johnny Taylor, Booker T. and the MGs, Carla Thomas, and, arguably the label's most impressive star of all, Otis Redding. Gaines got to know these and all the other artists who were so essential to the influential rhythm and blues and rock and roll recordings being produced at Stax Records during this period. In those early days at Stax, Gaines witnessed sessions by Otis Redding, Eddie Floyd, Sam and Dave, and the other mainstays who, by the end of the 1960s, had made the label a powerhouse in the pop and soul music world.

"If an artist came in, the in-house writers would write for them, or with them," Gaines explains. "For instance, Isaac Hayes and David Porter would go to the studio in the afternoon or later at night to write and demo their songs. I was usually given the job of recording some of these demo sessions. As they were writing, anyone might be playing whatever instrument was needed to just get the ideas recorded so they would be remembered when it came time to track. Then the MGs would come in and cut the songs, often turning out a pair of A sides and a pair of B sides at the same time. When they had cut enough tracks, they compiled them into an album. A lot of times the recordings were done in one pass, because they only had four tracks or mono to work with.

"One of the things I remember most was this huge speaker from the movie theater that Jim Stewart would listen to. It was right in front of him. That thing was big!

"Another thing I remember was that if there was any mixing or cutting going on and they needed reverb, they used the bathroom for an echo chamber. That meant you couldn't use that bathroom while they were working. It was primitive, but it worked. Another memory I have was when Isaac would come in. He would be wearing some interesting clothes combinations. He might have an orange shirt with purple pants. He and David Porter were a great writing team. David was always dressed up as well.

"Seeing and working with Albert King was a great experience as well," Gaines continues. "I got to work on one of his B sides. Likewise, watching the recording of some of Otis Redding and Carla Thomas's King and Queen album was pretty memorable. I don't think Carla and Otis were together for some of the duets. I do remember working on the demo of Little Johnny Taylor's song 'Who's Making Love to Your Old Lady?' before it was cut. I thought then, 'This song is a hit,' and it was." Indeed, Taylor's breakout single reached the number 1 position on Billboard's Hot R&B Singles chart and number 5 on the Billboard Hot 100 in the summer of 1968.

"When Otis [Redding] was in town," Gaines says, "he and Steve Cropper would grab a couple of guitars and rent a room at the Lorraine Hotel, where they would set up a writing room just for the two of them.

"When Otis was ready to cut some tracks, Atlantic Records' producer and engineer Tom Dowd would come in from New York and oversee the tracking. Tom had come down earlier to help out when they had some equipment problems, and he helped get them up and running again. Jim Stewart did a lot of the engineering early on, but as I recall, Dowd did it mostly for Otis. I recall one session with Otis where the Memphis Horns set up in one space, the band on the floor, and Otis and his background singers were set up behind some tall baffles, all singing next to one another. They were all recording live in a single take.

"Stax had a couple of different labels, and I think it was because of their deal with Atlantic [Records, founded in New York in 1947 by Ahmet Ertegun and Herb Abramson]. I wasn't privy to the business dealings, but there were other artists coming in from Atlantic to record as well. When Atlantic realized that Stax had a lot of [Redding] masters, they wanted to get them to New York. After Otis's death, the chief engineer called me at Tanner and asked if we had more than one four-track. I said we did. We were the only studio in town with two four-track machines. So he flew down and we spent two days making multiple copies of all the Otis masters and anything else that belonged to them. They shipped tapes several different ways for safety's sake. I kept one copy there until they had arrived safely.

"I'm pretty sure Wilson Pickett recorded there at some time," Gaines says. "There had been some problems with the sessions. One of the last things I remember doing [at Stax] is the live European recordings from Paris. Everyone was very proud of those shows." Indeed, the Stax tour of Europe in 1967, featuring performances by Otis Redding, Sam and Dave, and other Stax artists, is often credited with the worldwide breakout in the popularity of soul music.

Along with the triumphs, there were tragedies as well. Gaines still has vivid memories of the night when the airplane Otis Redding and his band were on crashed and killed nearly everyone on board.

"I'll never forget that night," Gaines says. "I walked in the studio and everyone was looking sad and worried. I asked what was going on and was told that Otis's plane was missing and they couldn't find it. He was flying to Madison, Wisconsin, to do a show, and somehow the plane went down and landed in a lake, and no one knew if there were any survivors. The Bar-Kays were his backing band on that tour. Sadly, only one person survived: Ben Cauley, the trumpet player. Another band member, James Alexander, had missed the flight. They were the only ones left alive in the band. I had done some mixing on one of their B sides just prior to that."

Gaines left Pepper-Tanner in 1969, and before his departure, the company had tried to start a record label. Marty Lacker, one of Elvis Presley's inner circle—sometimes known as the "Memphis Mafia"—was asked to run it. One of the acts he signed was Rita and Priscilla Coolidge.

"They recorded a couple of songs but had no promotion or distribution setup," Gaines remembers. "So nothing happened. Priscilla eventually became Booker's wife, and Rita went on to become a great artist in her own right."

His time at Pepper-Tanner, and perhaps more importantly at Stax Records, had afforded Jim Gaines the opportunity to begin developing into a seasoned studio engineer. In fact, when he became associated with Stax, Jim Gaines was tapping into an even earlier history of success and innovation in popular music recording, one that would form an important foundation for his long and successful career.

CHAPTER 3

On the Tracks with Stax

1960S

BY THE TIME JIM GAINES came on board, Stax Records already had a long and prosperous history. The label began life in 1957 as Satellite Records, operating in its earliest days out of a garage and focusing mainly on the country music and rockabilly rhythms that were popular and prevalent in the late 1950s. In fact, the music Satellite was recording reflected the influence of its owner, Jim Stewart, a fiddle player turned entrepreneur. A year later, Stewart's sister, Estelle Axton, invested $2,500 in the enterprise, using the proceeds of a loan secured by a mortgage on her family home.

Satellite subsequently relocated to Brunswick, Tennessee, moving into a small recording studio powered by an Ampex monaural console tape recorder bought with Axton's investment. Producer Chips Moman, who was on staff at that time, started steering the company away from country to a sound more akin to rhythm and blues, which eventually resulted in Satellite's first hit, "Fool in Love," by a group called the Veltones. The song is little more than a footnote in music history these days, but it did provide Stewart with an introduction to the man who would become the most successful star in the young days of the company, Memphis disc jockey and soul singer Rufus Thomas. When Satellite relocated operations to Memphis and the old Capitol Theater at 926 East McLemore Avenue, Thomas and his daughter Carla became the first artists to record there. The song that resulted from one of those sessions, "'Cause I Love

You," gave the company its first major success, selling some forty thousand copies. On the strength of this hit, Satellite was also able to ink a distribution deal with Atco, a subsidiary of Ahmet Ertegun's Atlantic Records.

The song's success also confirmed Stewart's decision to focus on soul music and rhythm and blues, the sound that would be identified with the company from 1961 onward. As national distributor, Atlantic had first option on the company's releases, but their broad reach also brought the company's small stable of artists to national prominence. An instrumental called "Last Night" by a newly signed group that originally called itself the Royal Spades—later renamed the Mar-Keys—brought even more attention when it crossed over into the top 5 on both the pop and R&B charts.

With success and nationwide airplay came unforeseen consequences, however. A California company, alleging that it had a copyright on the Satellite moniker, brought a complaint against Stewart's company. As a result, Stewart and Axton changed the name of their label to Stax, a combination of the first two letters of each of their last names.

Despite the name change, Stax continued increasing in national prominence. The label's house band, consisting primarily of members of Booker T. and the MGs (featuring Booker T. Jones on keyboards, Steve Cropper on guitar, drummer Al Jackson, and bassist Donald "Duck" Dunn), became a virtual hit-making machine and also began breaking down the racial divide in music as a fully integrated ensemble. The musicians would also provide the backing for every song Stax cut between 1962 and 1970. Having the services of seasoned and proven studio musicians who were well accustomed to performing with each other was a rare advantage for any recording company at the time. In addition, the in-house writing team, consisting of Jones, Cropper, and the talented duo of Isaac Hayes and David Porter, kept Stax well stocked with hits.

The studio itself also became a mecca for top talent. The sloped floors of the old movie theater created an unusual audio anomaly that came to define the Stax sound. Producer Tom Dowd's arrival in 1963 coincided with the studio's acquisition of the stereo recording capability that would replace the company's reliance on older, monaural technology. Stewart originally rejected the idea of stereo, fearing that the familiar and popular Stax sound would suffer. However, Dowd eventually won out, and two years after his arrival, he replaced the company's old Ampex mono recorder with a two-track deck that enabled sessions to be recorded in both mono and stereo at the same time. By the time Gaines arrived in late 1966, the system had been upgraded to four-track.

Estelle Axton's record store was set up by the building entrance and eventually expanded to the next-door space when the previous tenant, a barbershop, vacated the premises. The store sold records from rival labels as well as from Stax, and as Gaines recalls, it served several purposes: the store offered the younger members of the staff extra employment when times were lean; it provided a forum for Estelle to offer advice and encouragement to the label's talent; and it served as a kind of test market for the latest sounds in the marketplace.

The arrival of Otis Redding at the label in 1962 gave Stax a tremendous boost. By that time, the company had spun off a sister label, Volt, in an attempt to alleviate the appearance of a monopoly on top R&B talent. Beginning with his first Volt hit, "These Arms of Mine," released in October 1962, Redding enjoyed a steady succession of chart toppers, some seventeen in all. Other Stax artists helped stoke the momentum as well, including Carla Thomas and Booker T. and the MGs. When Stax renewed its distribution agreement with Atlantic/Atco in 1965, the presence of Stax and Volt artists on the hit charts increased with greater consistency.

But prosperity can be a two-edged sword, as Jim Gaines was about to learn. Stax was well established as a soul and R&B powerhouse, and that success ushered in other changes that were less enjoyable, in certain cases. However, Gaines had secured invaluable experience and witnessed firsthand what can happen when abundant musical talent finds a hospitable recording, promotional, and marketing environment. His time at Stax had prepared him for the new opportunities that were about to come his way.

CHAPTER 4

From Stax to TMI

1968–1970

WHEN ALVERTIS "AL" ISBELL, a former deejay, record producer, and songwriter, was brought in to oversee promotions operations at Stax in 1965, it marked a shift away from the homegrown, companionable mode of operation that had characterized the label since its beginnings. Certainly, Isbell helped nurture a new stable of stars, including the Staple Singers, Isaac Hayes, the Emotions, and the Dramatics. By the time he had been at Stax for ten years, he would be credited with successfully transforming the company into the second-largest African American–owned business in the United States.

Nevertheless, from Gaines's point of view, the label as he had known it was totally transformed, and not in a way he favored. "At one point Stax was sold to Gulf and Western, and the whole dynamic changed," he recalls. "The new company had a persistent demand for more product releases. We began cutting new albums in record time, both literally and figuratively."

In Gaines's opinion, the mom-and-pop atmosphere at Stax that he had found so appealing had all but disappeared. The label's partnership with Atlantic Records came to an end and a new corporate mentality took hold. Isbell began vying with Jim Stewart for influence. Cropper, meanwhile, also became dissatisfied, and when an offer came from Columbia Records chief executive Clive Davis to produce records exclusively for Columbia's offshoot

Epic, Cropper took the deal. Soon he started a recording operation of his own and embarked on a new career with a promise of prosperity.

Jim Gaines was still working part time at Stax while also overseeing studio operations at Pepper-Tanner, the jingle company.

"One day we were enjoying happy hour beer at Pappy's Lobster Shack, a hangout in Midtown [an area of Memphis] and a meeting place for some of the Pepper-Tanner employees, when I got a call from Steve Cropper asking me to come over to his new place for a meeting," Gaines remembers. "The studio was only a few blocks away. As he was showing me around his new studio, he told me that Denny Cordell, a noted British producer and hotshot with Shelter Records, was in town to record one of his acts. They had been working at another studio in town for a week, but unfortunately, the studio's owner had accidentally erased everything they had recorded. Needless to say, he wasn't happy, but he decided to start from scratch, and Cropper's studio was where he decided to do it."

Gaines learned that Cropper's studio hadn't officially opened, but he was trying to get everything in place to accommodate Cordell's emergency request. He had called a New York engineer to come down and help oversee the sessions, but that plan had fallen through. He needed a skilled engineer, and he asked Gaines whether he could work with Cordell in the evenings after he got off work at Pepper-Tanner. "He wanted me to start that night," Gaines said.

Gaines went to the sessions every night for an entire week, and after the tracks were completed, Cordell took them back to his studio in Tulsa, where Shelter's operations were based. A few weeks later, Gaines got another call from Cropper. The next engineer he had tried to hire wasn't working out, and he asked if Gaines wanted the position.

"It wasn't an easy decision," Gaines says. "I had a lot invested in Pepper-Tanner, including a management position and a company car. I told Steve and his partners what I would need to make the move, and they agreed. So, I gave my notice to Pepper-Tanner and began working for Cropper's company, which was called Trans Maximus Incorporated, or TMI for short."

Cropper had already put together a house band, and with the addition of young writers, he was soon able to assemble a production house similar to what Stax had been in its earlier days. One of TMI's initial projects was an Eddie Floyd album. Gaines enjoyed working on it, partly because it reunited him with Cropper, whom he had met while working at Stax. Although

Cropper was under contract to CBS Records, he was allowed to also work with Stax artists individually. In fact, although Cropper had officially departed Stax in 1970, he still had an office at the label, as well as an assistant.

"When I started at TMI, I had the opportunity to work with some great artists," Gaines reminisces. "We did some sessions with Roy Head, who had the hit 'Treat Her Right' [released in 1965, charting at number 2 on the pop and R&B lists]. He was full of fun, and his energy and enthusiasm were contagious.

"We also recorded a guy named Eric Mercury, a great singer who went on to write hits for Roberta Flack and Donny Hathaway. We also worked with Dreams in their formative stages. At that point they were a young supergroup of sorts, because their early lineup included the Brecker Brothers [trumpet player Randy, an original member of Blood, Sweat, and Tears; and saxophonist Michael], bassist Will Lee, Barry Rogers, John Abercrombie, Bob Mann, and George Cobham. I think it was their second album. Their sound was a combo jazz-rock sound. Great players.

"One of the oddest things I remember is when we worked with Sarah, a young woman from Texas who came to us after recording an entire album in LA that got scrapped entirely. Epic came to us and asked us to redo the record with her from scratch. They wanted a more down-home, rock sound."

Meanwhile, Cropper had signed some young local talent that he began prepping for recording purposes. At the same time, he began focusing on some of the artists CBS had in mind. One of the first projects TMI did under its arrangement with the label was *From the Inside*, the third album by the country-rock band Poco [Richie Furay, formerly of Buffalo Springfield; Jim Messina, who would later release major hits in partnership with Kenny Loggins; and Rusty Young, who also recorded with Buffalo Springfield], and its first to feature new singer and guitarist Paul Cotton. Like any group signed to CBS or one of its affiliates, Poco was obligated to work exclusively with CBS engineers because of union rules.

"Our closest CBS engineers were in Nashville," Gaines explains. "Now, Cropper and his partner Jerry Williams knew this, but it was decided that Poco would be getting to town a couple of days early and we would start the album on our own until the Nashville people showed up. We cut two songs before they arrived.

"Well, they weren't too happy that we had started without them. They even threatened to cut the tape off the reel. In truth, we had hoped that we could continue cutting the record while they were there and it would be enough that they were simply present. We considered it strictly a formality. But these guys thought otherwise. It took some negotiations, but eventually they agreed to let us keep our tracks and continue cutting the record."

The arrangement proved to be somewhat awkward. Gaines would get the sound he wanted from the board, but then when it came time to cut, the CBS engineer would slide in before the tapes started to roll. Cropper, who was producing the session, had Gaines sit next to him so that if any changes had to be made, the recording would stop to allow him to intervene. Meanwhile, the CBS engineer would slide out, wait for the fixes to be made, and then come back in when the production was again ready to roll.

"Eventually we all became friends and everything worked out," Gaines says. "As a matter of fact, the guys were so happy with me that after I moved to San Francisco, the CBS people in Nashville called and asked me to come to Nashville to do some work with them."

For its part, TMI always seemed to be busy. Oftentimes recording sessions would last until dawn. "Sometimes we would go have breakfast and then go home," Gaines remembers. "However, one time, I suggested we go fishing at a lake next to some property I owned in Mississippi, close to the Tennessee state line. I suggested to Steve that we grab some poles and go to the lake. Bear in mind that some of the longer sessions involved alcohol consumption, especially in the later hours. That likely influenced our decision to go by my house, get some fishing poles, and then continue to the lake. Naturally, we didn't tell anyone about it, including our wives. So there we were on the bank, with a bunch of poles in the water, all of us on our backs and eventually passed out. When we finally woke up, we were pretty badly sunburned, and all our poles were in the middle of the lake.

"By this time, everyone had started looking for us. When my wife found that the fishing poles were missing, she had someone from the studio go out looking for us. They found us around the time we were waking up. From that point on, we weren't allowed to go fishing again."

Gaines mentioned other distractions in the work environment. He relates that someone decided that one of the restrooms at the studio needed to be decorated, and subsequently the walls and ceiling were covered with pictures cut from the pages of *Playboy* magazine.

"Some of the guys took a lot of long bathroom breaks," Gaines laughs.

Gaines had enjoyed most of the circumstances of his time at TMI and especially liked working with Steve Cropper. But he found other factors less agreeable.

A year or so earlier, he had begun receiving an increased number of calls from Wally Heider, owner of a pair of popular studios in Los Angeles and San Francisco. To this point, Gaines had turned down several offers to move to the West Coast. But Heider was persistent, and now he was calling to offer Gaines a position in his San Francisco studios. Given his partial dissatisfaction with TMI, Gaines agreed to come take a look.

CHAPTER 5

San Francisco Beckons

1970

GAINES STILL CONSIDERS HIS DECISION to work for Wally Heider in San Francisco as most critical to his career. He immediately began recording artists who had recently been signed to major record labels and, as a result, found himself producing records for a new generation of performers bound for the top of the charts. It was a fortunate decision in other ways: after he left Memphis, the city's recording industry began taking a downward turn. Stax ended up on the sale block, and in-house producer Chips Moman moved his studio to Nashville, as did several of the city's recording facilities. Pepper-Tanner, the jingle company, was sold and eventually folded. TMI stayed in business for a few more years before closing.

Clearly, Gaines's move had come at the right time. But this wasn't the first time Wally Heider had tried to hire him. Two years earlier, he had contacted Gaines about coming to work for him in Los Angeles. Gaines had declined, insisting that there was no way he would want to raise his kids there. A year later, Heider, who was traveling from the West Coast to Nashville, called again and asked him to meet for lunch at the airport in Memphis.

"During that lunch he asked me again if I would consider working for him," Gaines says. "And again I told him my thoughts on moving to LA. At the end of lunch he gave me a gift, one of those great Bulova watches that allows you to see its gears moving inside. He said to me, 'Every time you look at this watch, it will say to you, 'Wally wants you to work for him.' I had that watch a long time."

Heider's next contact came when Gaines had been with TMI for a little over a year. This time, he caught Gaines at a particularly propitious time; Gaines was having doubts about whether he wanted to stay with the company. "I loved Cropper but had mixed feelings about other partners," he says in retrospect.

This time, Heider was calling from a vault that held archives of early German music. He was making copies of the very first taped recordings by some of the country's pioneering big bands. Heider was a big band historian, and his entrance into the music industry had been precipitated by that specific interest. He was originally a lawyer but had always loved mingling with musicians. Heider made Gaines a gift of some archival albums from his private collection, an offering Gaines still cherishes. Consequently, when Heider called and mentioned he needed someone for his San Francisco studio, Gaines agreed to fly out and take a look.

There were three studios in Heider's new location. One had been dedicated for the use of Jefferson Airplane. When they weren't using the studio, Heider and his team had full access.

As it turned out, one reason Heider wanted Gaines to work for him was that his current studio manager was planning to retire in a couple of years, and Heider believed Gaines had the management experience needed to replace him. Gaines was asked to audition by doing a mix of a previously recorded song. They gave him approximately an hour to mix the track to see whether he would get a good result in a limited amount of time.

The song happened to be by one of the hottest bands of the era and one of Gaines's favorite bands of all time, Creedence Clearwater Revival. The song had been recorded at Heider's, and at the time, Russ Gary, a Heider employee who had recorded the earlier Creedence albums, was moving over to Fantasy Studios, which CCR's label had built to give John Fogerty a studio exclusively for the band's use. Naturally, then, Fantasy wanted Russ to be its in-house producer and engineer, so in addition to the retirement of his studio manager, Heider also needed a replacement for Gary.

"After I did the mix and we all had a listen, I was not only asked if I wanted the job, but how soon could I be there," Gaines recalls. "I struck a great deal for myself. I even managed to secure five weeks of paid vacation after the first year, as well as a percentage of the studio billing." Gaines told Heider he would be there in five weeks, explaining that he had to sell his house and get ready to drive out west with his family.

0000000

Once Gaines arrived in San Francisco, one of the first sessions he was involved with was overdubbing strings for a recording conducted by Ray Brown. It was a union gig, so everything had to go perfectly to avoid racking up overtime. Gaines found such sessions nerve-racking, because they normally went from 9:00 a.m. until noon and then, after a lunch break, continued from 1:00 p.m. until an indefinite time later that night. Because the cheapest times to record were in the morning, Gaines found himself working two or three sessions a day while also keeping a close eye on the clock, since he was directly responsible for controlling overhead costs.

It was around that time that Gaines also began working with a new horn-oriented band called Tower of Power. He recalls doing some of the final demos they recorded prior to landing a deal with Warner Bros. Records. The band happened to be big fans of Stax Records and Steve Cropper in particular. As a result, once they signed with the label, they asked Cropper to produce their album. Ironically, they decided to record at TMI, the studio with which Gaines had recently parted ways.

Unfortunately, Cropper was under contract to CBS and couldn't officially produce Tower of Power, because they were a Warner Brothers act. By this time, Gaines's former colleague Ronnie Capone had left Stax to take Gaines's place at TMI. Consequently Capone was named the official producer for Tower of Power. However, once the recording was finished, Cropper called Gaines and asked him to redo a few more lead vocal tracks on the song called "Still a Young Man." They sent him the tapes, and Gaines recorded several takes with Rick Stevens. The song ended up as a lead single and became a radio hit, peaking at number 29 on the *Billboard* Hot 100.

Not surprisingly, then, when Tower of Power got ready to do their next album, they asked Gaines to record it. "They said, 'Why should we go to Memphis when Memphis is right here?'" Gaines notes. "They gave me the nickname 'Memphis Slim.' I was pretty skinny in those days."

Gaines did three more albums with Tower of Power. "The first album we did was an adventure," he says. "First of all, Tower of Power didn't have a keyboard player. When they were in Memphis, they used a blind, in-house keyboardist named Jay Spell. So when we started the second album, they wanted Jay to come out and put some parts on.

"We're working on the album and getting close to finishing it when three of the band members decided not to show up for a couple of the gigs. Emilio, the band's leader, was naturally upset. They had a meeting in the control room with the manager, trying to figure out what to do. They decided to fire the errant players and start the project over again. Warner Brothers was okay with that. So new players were brought in: guitarist Bruce Conte, singer Lenny Williams, and saxophonist Lenny Pickett.

"While we were working on the album—doing horns, I think—they put out a call to a keyboard player named Chester Thompson. They were going to audition him in a vacant studio while we worked. We got a call to come down and listen. Wow, was he good! He got hired that night. Chester and I had a thirty-year relationship. He later became part of the Santana band as well," Gaines recalls.

"While doing or redoing the first Tower project, an unusual thing happened," Gaines continues. "We were in the middle of working one night when Doug, the road manager, walks in. He says, 'Stop the session!' He had been diagnosed with possible hepatitis, he told us, which meant we all had been exposed to it. We're thinking, 'Great!'

"He called the hospital and made arrangements for us to go and get shots, so we piled into taxis. When we get there, they take us to a larger exam room. This lady doctor comes in and has us line up along this long counter and drop our pants. She brings out this very big needle full of medicine. This shot is one that takes a little while to dispense and it goes way into your butt. I'm the last one to get it. So here we were all lined up, with our behinds showing. When we got back to the studio, I asked Doug if he had gotten a picture of this. Because, believe it or not, the song we were working on right then was titled 'Soul Vaccination.' That image could have been the back cover shot if someone had taken it."

"Tower of Power is one of the best horn sections I have ever recorded," he says. "I still love those guys."

While in San Francisco, Gaines also worked on a Blue Thumb record compilation of Bay Area bands. Tower of Power was included, as well as Dan Hicks and the Hot Licks, Sylvester, and a group called Cold Blood. Gaines still professes his admiration for its singer, Lydia Pense.

000

Gaines then worked with a duo from Kansas City called Brewer and Shipley. It was after their big hit "One Toke over the Line," and Gaines went on to do their next two albums. "They were great writers and vocalists," he remembers. "Working with them, I got a chance to meet and work with some of the great folk-rock musicians in town: people like Nick Gravenites and Mark Naftalin.

"We recorded one album live at the famous Cowtown Ballroom in Kansas City," Gaines continues. "I remember that the place was so packed, that when you went into the men's restroom, there would be women there waiting in line with the guys; they said the wait was too long in their restroom.

"Ozark Mountain Daredevils was opening for Brewer and Shipley. They actually ended up getting signed that night by Glyn Johns for A&M Records."

0000000

One of the most significant projects Gaines was involved in was Van Morrison's landmark album *Saint Dominic's Preview*. "Working with Van was a trip," Gaines says. "First, we had a normal vocal booth to put singers in while we were tracking in order to get a separation of sound. So here I am, setting up the booth, and Van comes in and tells me he's not going in there. He wants to stand in front of the drums and play and sing with the background singers next to him.

"It was an engineering nightmare. You simply couldn't get any separation between the vocalists and the drums. But that's what he wanted to do, so that's what I gave him.

"The arranger on the session was someone I had worked with before. With no separation because of the setup Van wanted, I explained what to expect when it came time to mix, but he told me to go with it, regardless.

"When Van came into the control room to listen back, he would say something about the performance, but because of his Irish accent and the fact he was slurring his words, I really couldn't understand a word he was saying. Tom, the arranger, had to translate for me all night."

Ultimately, it didn't matter. The music translated well enough.

000

The impressive variety of musicians Gaines worked with during his time with Heider in San Francisco included Alexis Korner, a British blues pioneer who, like John Mayall, gave a lot of budding British blues musicians their start, including members of the Rolling Stones. The backup band was the King Crimson rhythm section. "They were a great group, and he was one of the greatest blues players I ever worked with," Gaines recalls.

Gaines also enjoyed working with Dave Mason [formerly of Traffic]. "That boy could play some guitar," Gaines insists. "He had a great drummer with him. We only did a few cuts, but that was a great session."

Quicksilver Messenger Service was one of the more prominent Bay Area bands in the late sixties and early seventies, so it was no surprise that they made a pretty profound impression on Gaines as well. "Guitarist John Cipollina was a great player, but the first night I met him, he was wearing makeup and what seemed like a cape. Where I came from, not many men wore makeup. Nevertheless, the band was good, and I ended up working with several of the band members on separate projects."

Gaines also ended up working with composer and pianist Vince Guaraldi on one of his *Peanuts* television specials. "I think it was the Thanksgiving special," Gaines recalls. "Vince was one of the premier jazz piano players and such a nice guy [Guaraldi is also the composer and performer of the jazz standard "Cast Your Fate to the Wind"]. We didn't have video hookup in those days, so we were winging it on the tracks. He created the signature sound that's used to this day on those shows. I'll never forget that big old smile of his."

000

Gaines remembers one particular project that wasn't nearly as easy as working with the good-natured Vince Guaraldi. Paul Kantner and Grace Slick from Jefferson Airplane had embarked on a solo project called *Baron Von Tollbooth and the Chrome Nun*, which would eventually evolve into their new amalgam, Jefferson Starship.

"The sessions would start the same way every night," Gaines recalls. "The road crew would come in with a large garbage bag full of pot, followed by enough cocaine to fill one of those brown glass ashtrays that usually sit in a stand. There were also cases of beer and Grace's favorite wine.

"Sometimes Grace would come in and tell the crew that she had left her car running in the middle of the street, and someone needed to deal with it." Gaines notes that the studio was in a part of San Francisco known as the Tenderloin—not a safe place to leave a car unlocked with the keys inside, much less still running. "That meant that someone from the crew had to race out to get it before someone got in her car and actually took off with it.

"I remember one time when Paul Kantner got so upset with something that he came flying into the control room and then proceeded to kick the thermostat off the wall. I'm thinking, 'Great, what do we do now?' Another time

I recall Grace playing piano, and although she was pretty good, I kept hearing this clicking sound coming into the mics. I went out to see what it was and discovered it was her long fingernails hitting the keys. So I said to her very gingerly, 'Grace, you may have to trim your nails.' Of course, no woman who cares about her nails wants to hear that. So we were stuck with those clicks on the track.

"While all this craziness was going on, we had a couple of visiting engineers from another studio who had also wanted to be working on the project but were instead simply hanging out. They kept making suggestions as to how we should record and what equipment we should use. After a few days of this, I went to my boss, explained the situation, and asked to be taken off the project. It wasn't what I needed in my life. So I took myself out of the situation."

Of course, San Francisco was the home of another iconic group, the Grateful Dead. Gaines was familiar with the band because they had once worked in an adjoining studio.

"So here I am, booked for a Dead session," Gaines says. "I start setting up mics for the band, when in walks Rocky, the road manager. He informs me that the band isn't coming, but they are going to use the studio anyway. He gives me a Dead album and tells me to get a turntable and take down the mics.

"I did what was asked, and then in comes the road crew and their ladies carrying two tanks of nitrous oxide with about twelve tubes coming out of them. My session turned into me playing the album over and over again while they all got high on laughing gas. It ended with several of the guys getting into a fight over someone paying too much attention to someone else's wife."

Summing up these experiences, Gaines deadpans, "Isn't music such fun sometimes?"

CHAPTER 6

A Period of Proficiency

1970

GAINES WAS FULLY ENGAGED at Wally Heider's studio in San Francisco when his past came calling. He was about to return to his roots but in an unlikely new location.

"My old boss at Pepper-Tanner, Weldon Jetton, and another engineer had started a custom recording console business," he recalls. "They had built the boards for Stax and TMI as well as for other studios. What had begun as a side business eventually turned into a full-time occupation. After being at Heider's for about year, I got a call from Weldon asking me if I would consider moving to Dallas to run and be the partial owner of a studio he was building.

"At this point, I was doing two sessions a day for Heider—a pretty heavy workload. I asked Weldon about the gear that he was installing and the business he would be looking for. He replied that he would go after the jingle business, at least in part, but that he also wanted me to bring in rock business.

"I told him I wasn't keen about going back to the jingle business but agreed to keep in touch and keep talking and see how it played out. But somehow he got the idea that I would be coming there. Remember, at Heider's, we had the latest gear, and the clients were used to high-end recording sessions. Dallas wasn't known as a bastion of rock; it was only a place to do jingles at that point. So the more we talked, the more I got the impression that the gear would be both lower in quality and quantity. Then, when I got a call one morning after an all-night session and he told what the final gear would be, I just couldn't believe it. Definitely not worth leaving Heider's. I had to tell him that it wasn't what I expected, and I had to pass on his offer. He almost cried. As it turned out, Weldon's studio only remained in business about two years. Here again, my timing worked out for the best, thank goodness."

000

Meanwhile, Gaines was stacking up a series of great sessions at Heider's. He has fond memories of working with Sal Valentino, one of the singers and songwriters with the legendary San Francisco group the Beau Brummels. It began with a phone call from Tom Donahue, the groundbreaking deejay who programmed KSAN radio in San Francisco. He happened to be managing a band called Stoneground, which Valentino had founded following the breakup of the Beau Brummels. The band included several lead singers who had been assembled as part of a movie deal.

"Sal was a great player and singer, and with the girls added, they were a great vocal band," Gaines recalls. "But the girls picked on me a lot and would tease me by asking me to speak with some southern slang. When I obliged, they would laugh their asses off. They saw me as some kind of novelty. Because I had never done drugs, they decided I needed an experience. So they offered me some 'special' brownies. I loved sweets then and I love sweets now, but I had no idea they had laced these brownies with marijuana. I ate a portion of one, and luckily I didn't eat any more. Even so, it was all I could do to hold myself together for the remainder of the session. The girls thought it was hilarious. From that point on, I was very wary anytime anyone offered me cookies or baked goods."

000

Gaines has fond memories of a session with musician Turk Murphy, who owned a club in San Francisco called Earthquake McGoon's. The club's basement housed a museum filled with magic memorabilia, mainly from a performer named Carter the Great.

Murphy was considered one of the world's great Dixieland trombonists. Prior to meeting Gaines, he already had twenty albums to his credit. Gaines's big band session experiences made him an obvious choice to work with Murphy.

"We were working in a small room, which made it difficult to record vocals at the same time," Gaines explains. "So I asked if we could bring back his singer and overdub the vocals. The morning the singer arrived for the session, it was clear that she was not only nervous, but had also been drinking.

"One of the first songs we worked on that morning was 'Rose of Washington Square,' a song about a 'lady of the night.' The singer was an older woman, slightly overweight, and she had dressed quite elaborately as well. I turned the lights down to make her more comfortable. As she started singing the song, I looked up and saw that she was stripping as she was singing. Turk looked over at me and we both started cracking up. We actually had to duck behind the console so she couldn't see us. By the time we got to the end of the song, most of her clothes were gone. That's when we decided we probably shouldn't do another take. I've seen a lot of things while recording, but that's one session I'll never forget."

Gaines did two albums with Murphy. Several years later, representatives from the Jazz Preservation Society called and asked whether he would record Murphy one last time. Murphy was in failing health, but he wanted no one but Gaines for what would probably be his final recording session. Unfortunately, Gaines was in the middle of a project at the time. He promised he would do it as soon as he could and assured the society that he really wanted to produce the recording. Sadly, though, he didn't make it in time, and Murphy passed away before the two men could reconnect. "I regretted not being able to do that for him," Gaines says.

000

Wally Heider's San Francisco studio was not in the best part of town, and Gaines says that every once in a while, some interesting characters would arrive at the front door. His new car was vandalized once and stolen on another occasion.

"A funny thing happened two weeks after my car was stolen," Gaines recalls. "I was walking over to get my rental vehicle, and a car pulls into the lot. A couple of guys get out and break into another car, right as I'm watching. I quickly went back to the studio and called the police. After they showed up, I explained what had just happened. They then take off to the lot around the corner. In the meantime, one of our engineers and a friend of his had pulled into the lot and started smoking a joint. The police spotted them as they came flying around the corner, pulled them out of their car, and started searching them. As I came around the corner to get my car, the guys are yelling to me and asking for help. I had to explain to the cops that these weren't the guys who broke into the car. Fortunately, the police let them go. Needless to say, my friend thanked me profusely for showing up when I did."

Drug use in San Francisco was fairly prevalent but illegal, so as a precautionary measure, the studio had installed strobe lights inside a speaker cabinet in the corner of each room. "The idea was that if the police came in the front door, the receptionist could throw a switch that would turn those strobes on and warn the bands to get rid of their stash. One day, I'm working with a famous band and the lights go off. There was a mad rush to get to the bathroom so the musicians could flush everything down the toilet. Most of it was pot. Shortly thereafter, I get a call from the receptionist. She was crying and saying she had turned the switch on accidentally. She was mortified, and so were the musicians, because their pot was on its way to the sewers. As a result, we had to make up the cost for the lost drugs on behalf of two musicians. So, the overhead cost on that record went up a little bit, sort of unexpectedly."

000

Gaines has more enjoyable memories of a pair of projects with jazz great George Duke, who recorded with artists as diverse as Cannonball Adderley and Frank Zappa. One of them was a live in-studio recording for a German label Duke was signed with. Duke had a great band and he played a souped-up Fender Rhodes that produced a great sound. Gaines did several jazz projects while at Heider's, including some work with Herbie Hancock on a couple of albums that he and part of his rhythm section played on.

"Not many people know this, but aside from being superb musicians, Herbie and his bass player Paul Jackson were quite involved with Sony Japan in their research and development of the very first digital recorders," Gaines says. In the early seventies, Jackson had built a bass guitar that allowed each string to separately feed four amps directly at once. This was quite an advanced technique at the time. "Those two guys are very smart," Gaines insists. "They were also instrumental in coming up with a usable digital two-track recorder."

Gaines laughs at another recollection. "Once, while I was working with Herbie at the Automatt [a studio in San Francisco], we had our photo taken for *Mix* magazine. At that time, my Afro hairdo was bigger than his! That gave us a good reason to chuckle. Years later, when I worked with him and Santana at the Montreux Festival in Switzerland, I came up to him and said, 'Hey, dude, my 'fro is still bigger than yours.' He had lost most of his hair by then, but I couldn't help but point out that I still had most of mine."

Gaines also had an opportunity to work with Dr. Eddie Henderson, who, besides being an accomplished trumpet player with a record deal, was also a practicing doctor. During this time Gaines also worked with guitar innovator Lee Ritenour.

"Those were great sessions," Gaines says. "There were several heavyweight New York jazz guys involved. While doing one of these albums, one of the musicians and a lady friend went looking for a place in the studio where they could make out. They ended up sneaking into the live echo chamber, not realizing that there are two live mics on at all times. All of a sudden, as we're recording, we hear the sound of two of these voices coming over the speakers. It was clear that they were making out. We just paused our session and listened in on theirs, cracking up the whole time. When they came back to the control room, we stopped and gave them some great applause and a big cheer. I think they were pretty embarrassed."

Gaines recalls other "extracurricular" antics. "I had this new kid working for me who thought he knew everything," Gaines chuckles. "So, to mess with him, as I'm sometimes known to do, I put a cricket in his echo chamber while he was mixing. When it was dark in there, the cricket would holler, but when the lights were turned on to look for him, he stopped. It drove this guy crazy, trying to find him. I thought that was a lot of fun.

"To test these young engineers, I'd send them to the local electronics store to get what I called 'stereo razor blades.' Of course, there's no such thing as stereo razor blades, although the name sounds like there ought to be. The owner of the store called me one day and pleaded, 'Please don't send these kids down here anymore.' It embarrassed them so badly, because they thought they were real tools we needed for the session, even though they hadn't heard of them before. That got a lot of those kids trained right away. The humility was good for them."

000

After a while, Gaines gained a reputation as an expert in Dixieland jazz, R&B, and later, somewhat interestingly, as a belly dancing music specialist. Gaines admits he had never heard of belly dancing music before he got to San Francisco.

"The first album I did was with a traveling version of their music. One of the club owners on Broadway had hired this band to record with him as his backup band while they were in town. The arranger was well known in the genre, the equivalent of someone like Burt Bacharach, maybe. The band had Middle Eastern drums and violin, an oud [a lute-like instrument], and an instrument called a santoor, which is very much like an autoharp. It was supposedly one hundred years old. The band normally recorded with thirty musicians in a room and two mics. So I stereo-miked this santoor so that when it played back, it would walk across the speakers. It blew their minds. They had never heard anything like this before, so they thought I was some sort of genius. I didn't even know how to mix this music, but I gave it my best shot. They loved it.

"At the same time, the belly dancers would come to the studio and dance while we were recording. I enjoyed that. As it turned out, two other people wanted to record themselves with that band. I ended doing three albums and soon came to be known as a belly dancing music expert. It was interesting, because I got to work with instruments that I had never seen or heard of before. I also had to figure out how to create a mix that would properly balance the instruments. It all worked out."

Gaines also worked with a sitar player who, at the time, was similar in stature to Ravi Shankar, famous for his influence with the Beatles. "I had never seen this kind of instrument before, and of course I had no idea how to mike it. It's a very special, large instrument, so microphone placement was a little tricky. The session consisted of the sitar player and his drummers. The drummers played Middle Eastern drums and the sitar player sat in the middle of the floor while the other players sat on the floor surrounding him. It made for a very spiritual setting. The musicians would hold a short religious ceremony before we got started. The music was very emotional, and watching them play was an amazing experience. I still wasn't sure how to mix the music, but somehow I got through it. During this period of time, San Francisco was amazing for all the different musical styles that I was able to experience there."

000

Graham Nash, of the Hollies and Crosby, Stills, Nash, and Young, also sought out Gaines's prowess under unusual circumstances. "I was walking out of my session one night when Graham stopped me," Gaines recalls. "He and David Crosby were working in the studio next to me on a Crosby-Nash project. He asked if I was finished for the night, and when I said yes, he asked me if I could come and help them out for a while. I said, yes, of course. I went into their control room, and their engineer was passed out on the console—completely laid out. So we got him up and put him on the couch, and I ended up finishing the session for them. Graham was a sweet guy. I once got to go to his house, and I still remember his unusual but beautiful decor."

000

One of the artists that Gaines worked with on a compilation album for the Blue Thumb record label was Sylvester, a singer from a well-known drag group named Sylvester and the Hot Band. Sylvester played piano and sang, but when he came into the control room, Gaines noticed that he was wearing a see-through white gauze dress, full makeup, and a World War I aviator hat that had a flowing white ostrich plume sticking out of it.

"Where I came from, men didn't dress like that, especially in those days," Gaines remarks. "He had about twenty bracelets on one arm and a whole bunch on the other. One of the first things he says is, 'Oh, Jim, I have been looking forward to working with you.' Meanwhile, he's stroking my arm at the same time. Folks just didn't do that where I was raised. Eventually the room filled up with guys making out with guys and girls getting it on with girls. That was another new experience for me at that point. Finally we all got settled in and finished the recording, and I must say he played and sang great. We all loved working with each other. He ended up being a big early disco star. I'm not surprised—even though the way the session started was pretty surprising."

000

Gaines also recalls a surprising development related to a session with Stevie Wonder, who had come to the studio as a guest musician on a solo album by Greg Reeves, former bass player for Crosby, Stills, Nash, and Young. "Here I was, recording Stevie Wonder playing drums," Gaines marvels. "Yes, drums! He played them really well, which I guess should not be a surprise, since he reportedly played drums on several of his own albums.

"I was also present at a Stevie Wonder recording session in LA. One of my fellow engineers worked for Motown in Detroit and knew Stevie well. We were in Los Angeles for something or other and got invited over to watch the session. Stevie's room was set up for several different instruments, and one of them had a very big Moog synthesizer; this was in the early days when that instrument was first coming into use. Pepper-Tanner had been one of the first studios in the South to have one, actually. I had seen them at an AES [Audio Engineering Society] show once and decided we needed one for our jingles. That was actually one of the real reasons I wanted to see Stevie's setup. We got to say hello and see the Moog, but I didn't want to hang out and intrude on his session."

000

Gaines worked briefly with guitarist Mike Bloomfield, a once-famous session player who had also been instrumental in forming the supergroup Electric Flag and had gained further fame through his participation on the album *Super Session* with Stephen Stills and Al Kooper, which peaked at number 12 on the *Billboard* 200 and was later certified gold. "He was a great player, but he was kind of messed up, those two days," Gaines recalls. "We got something done, but it took a while. On the other hand, when he was on, he was amazing."

A session that fared better involved early demos of the band that later became known as Journey. Neal Schon and Gregg Rolie had just left Santana and were putting together their new group. At that point, the roster was still in a state of flux. "I remember them after the new band was finally put together, and they opened for Steve Miller. At that point they were more a rock-fusion style music. Later on I would work with them on their album *Raised on Radio*." The album, released in 1986, would spawn four high-charting singles and would be certified double platinum.

But as productive and prolific as his work had been while at Heider's, burnout eventually began to settle in for Jim Gaines. "I ended up working so many hours, often staying at a little hotel across the street that the studio had an arrangement with," he says. "It was an hour's drive back to my house, and sometimes I would only have a few hours between sessions. So instead of going home, I'd grab a room at the hotel and get a few hours' sleep. It helped, but I was working so many hours that my wife told me that she would return to Tennessee if I didn't slow down."

Around this time, Gaines received a call from the owners of Kaye-Smith Studios in Seattle. They were opening a new facility downtown. The owners were all notable individuals, the most prominent of whom was the well-known actor Danny Kaye. Other associates included Lester Smith, a successful business executive; and a local disc jockey, Pat O'Day. The group already owned six radio stations and one of the biggest concert promotion companies in the world, Concerts West.

Gaines decided to fly to Seattle one weekend to check things out. "You can't find anything much prettier on a clear day than a view of Puget Sound from the fourteenth floor of Washington Plaza. It was unbelievable," he says. With such favorable impressions, Gaines began making plans for a new phase in his already-rich career.

CHAPTER 7

Settled in Seattle

1973–1974

JIM GAINES MADE A LOT of weighty decisions in his lengthy career, but none was more so than his decision to move to Seattle to be a part of an important new venture.

Kaye-Smith Studios consisted of two rooms that had been designed by Tom Hidley, who was also famous for designing the two very successful Record Plant recording studios in New York and LA. In fact, the Seattle facilities marked the thirteenth studio he was involved with. Kaye-Smith aspired to create a record label and production company in the Northwest, complete with a major studio operation.

Gaines bought a house for his family in Kirkland, Washington, just across a lake from the studio. It was a beautiful setting, next to a big bridle-trail park. He was looking forward to slowing down and working at a less frenzied pace. Unfortunately, it didn't quite work out that way; the first week he was there he worked a total of eighty hours.

Gaines had brought with him the Tower of Power record he had started working on in San Francisco and mixed it at Kaye-Smith. Later, he would work on another Tower of Power album, *Back to Oakland*, which he would record in Seattle and mix at the Record Plant in Los Angeles.

Another band Gaines worked with was a funk horn band from Vancouver called the Sunshine Boys. The group was helmed by a Canadian artist named Bruce Fairbairn, who also happened to be a big Tower of Power fan. "We had a great time," Gaines recalls. "Later he became a big-time producer in Vancouver, responsible for a lot of hits."

As it turned out, Kaye-Smith wasn't the only studio operation in the Northwest. Vancouver had a major facility called Little Mountain Sound, which provided formidable competition and recorded albums by artists like Aerosmith, Bon Jovi, AC/DC, and many others. Mushroom Records, a company that originated in Australia, had a small studio there as well. However, Kaye-Smith's strategy was to attract Canadian clientele as well as artists based in the Pacific Northwest.

One of the first groups to take advantage of the studio was Heart, who came in to record what would be their sophomore album, *Little Queen*. "They were great," Gaines recalls. "Those women were talented."

Bachman-Turner Overdrive (BTO) came to the studio to record their *Not Fragile* album, which included the huge hits "Roll on Down the Highway" and "You Ain't Seen Nothing Yet." Kaye-Smith was convenient for the band; Randy Bachman lived nearby.

The studio had hired three engineers: one from New York, one from LA, and Gaines. "The idea was that each of us could bring some of our business with us, and of course bring our reputations as well," he explains. The engineer from LA was Richie Moore, an experienced studio pro who had worked for Wally Heider's location in Los Angeles. Buzz Richmond, from New York, had less experience than Gaines or Moore, though he was a highly qualified engineer.

"Richie Moore probably had the best ears of almost anyone I had known in my career up to that point," Gaines reflects. "I loved working with him, but he had what you might call a 'chemical enhancement' problem. And you never knew how the session could end up when he was at the console. One night about midnight, I got a call at home saying, 'Richie's out of control.' When I got to the studio, he was standing in the middle of the console, waving his arms. You don't stand on a very expensive console. So I told the people who were there to get him down, and I talked him into going home for the night. Some years later, he was working above the ceiling of a studio in San Rafael; it gave way and he fell through. He ended up bursting one of his eardrums, which ended his career as a mixer. I asked him to come and help me out several times after that, still doing some mixing, because even with just one ear, he was still damn good. Here was a kid who flew small jet planes at twenty-two years old. He was definitely a genius. I miss Richie. May he rest in peace."

000

Gaines was enthusiastic about the Kaye-Smith facility. He says the studio was well equipped with top-quality gear. "I was a kind of assistant manager. We also had a manager who was involved in filmmaking projects, because we not only did records but also videos. I remember that Danny Kaye stopped in at the sessions every once in a while. He was always dressed like he just walked off the golf course, and he was always fun to see. Once he came in and got behind the console, looked over at me, and asked, 'Do you know how to run all these knobs and switches?' I replied, 'Only on Tuesday and Thursday. So what day is it?'

"He burst out laughing. We always enjoyed it when he came over."

Gaines had the opportunity to work on several major projects while he was employed there. Along with Tower of Power, the studio was the site for recordings by other notable artists including the Spinners, Dionne Warwick, Steve Miller, and several prominent Canadian acts besides BTO.

One of the studio's biggest clients was Thom Bell of Mighty Three Productions in Philadelphia. He had moved to Tacoma because of his wife's medical problems. He brought with him several of his projects, including the Spinners, who ended up doing a pair of albums at Kaye-Smith Studios. Bell himself would commute to Philadelphia and record additional tracks with the rhythm section. Then he would fly back to Seattle and do overdubs and some of the mixing. Gaines got to work on most of Bell's projects. In fact, he received a gold record for the album *Happiness with the Spinners*. He also helped with the mixing for one of the group's live albums.

Gaines also worked with Dionne Warwick on *Track of the Cat*, released in 1975 on the Rhino Entertainment label. "One of the songs she was singing was about her recent breakup," Gaines mused. "Thom warned me that we might only get one take. I prepared several tracks with different levels, just in case something on levels didn't work out. We had the lights down low and a small music-stand light in the room. She started singing, and the more she got into it, the more emotional she became. When she finished singing, we all were crying. She had completely put her heart into that vocal.

"Later, I took Dionne and Thom to dinner at her hotel. We had a great time, because after all, we'd had a great session. When we were saying goodbye, she came up and kissed me on the cheek and said that no other engineer had treated her so well and then she thanked me again. She was such a nice lady, and she had such a great voice."

The Spinners sessions were memorable as well. "When we were doing their vocals, they all wanted to get around one mic and balance themselves for the recording. One of the guys was having nodes removed from his throat, so Philippe Wynne was brought in to cover for him until he was able to sing again. When one of the guys was struggling with a note, Thom would go out and sing it. Thom was a trumpet player but also the best tambourine player I ever worked with. He was so talented. I ended up getting a gold record for that project.

"One night Thom Bell and Don Murray were working on a mix and were having a hard time getting the right fade on the song. I was sitting behind them, watching, and I finally asked them to let me try. I nailed it right away, so after that I was known as the 'Fade King,'" Gaines says, laughing.

"Working with Thom was great because he was a real pro, always prepared, he could do it all. I have a lot of great memories to thank Thom for."

Marlin Green also joined the team at Kaye-Smith. He was from Muscle Shoals, Alabama, and had penned several hit records and worked in the artist and repertoire division for Elektra Records. As an A&R rep, he looked for talent and signed new acts. The company ended up with several local bands that recorded some demos and released some albums distributed by Bell Records. Unfortunately, the company couldn't officially own a record label because of a Federal Communications Commission policy that prohibited owners of radio stations (it had six) from also owning a record label, because of conflict of interest. That forced it to sign artists through a major label. Unfortunately, the label never took off, even though Green signed some good acts and the studio produced some good records.

000

Painter, a band from Calgary who had gone to Heider's in San Francisco to work with Gaines on one of their albums, followed Gaines to Seattle when it was time to record a new project. "Danny Lowe was the leader of the band," Gaines says. "Before going into the studio, I suggested that they rehearse in my garage. I'm sure my neighbors loved that. While recording the project, a couple of interesting things happened.

"First, we were trying to get a special room sound on the guitar amps. So one night we decided to put the amp in the women's bathroom. The women had left for the day, so we thought we could use it. As we're recording, we hear this big crash. We go in and discover we've blown the women's sanitary napkin machine off the wall. That was the end of our access to using the women's bathroom for recording purposes.

"It also happened that the bass player was the harmony singer in the band. He always wanted to sing the kind of notes you would need a ladder to reach. So he was singing away but not hitting the notes. He stopped and said, 'How can I get this part right, because one side of my phones is flat and one side is sharp.' We all looked at each other in disbelief. That would be impossible. Later he said the air conditioner vent was vibrating out of tune. Artists can find some pretty creative excuses for not getting their part right.

"When we were at the mixing stage of a song called 'West Coast Woman,' we had an equipment malfunction in the middle of it all. So we stopped and decided to take a break, going to Trader Vic's for some food and drinks. We ordered one of the rum drinks in a big bowl with six straws, and damn, it was potent. So by the time we got back to the job of finishing the mix, the rum had really kicked in. We finished the mix at dawn, and it ended up as the brightest mix I've ever done. It's too bad the tune was only a regional hit.

"The band ended up changing their name several times, but to this day, Painter still has a cult following. I've had several radio stations wanting to know if I have any of their albums. I ended up recording two or three more albums with them."

000

Amid all the recording activity, Kaye-Smith's owners decided they would bring a pro baseball team back to Seattle. They set up temporary offices at the studio until they could move into their own. They also wanted the public to help name the team, so they ran a contest in the newspaper, offering local people the opportunity to suggest some names. The winner would receive tickets to a game that first season.

"The best name I saw was 'The Seattle Wet Sox,'" Gaines chuckles. "Now, you can't get any better than that for a Seattle team. But they ended up as the Mariners. Shucks."

Gaines was exposed to local sports in another way when he was put in charge of recording pro basketball player Bill Russell's weekly radio show. "He was the tallest man I'd ever seen. He was also a great guy and lots of fun. I would get tickets to the Sonics games, sitting right behind the players. Being that close to the guys gives you an entirely different vantage point."

000

The production company also connected with some people in Los Angeles who were interested in doing a Bo Diddley record on spec, for which they could later shop around for distribution. They brought in some prime session players from LA to record the tracks, including Hal Blaine on percussion; Larry Knechtel on piano; Tim Bogert and Carmine Appice, formerly of Vanilla Fudge, on bass and drums, respectively; and Chris Bond to arrange and play some guitar.

"Bo wasn't there when we were cutting these seven or eight tracks," Gaines mentions. "After a couple days of tracking, we bring Bo in to listen and start his overdub parts. He comes in and sits beside me at the console to start listening. So I played the first track, and he looks at me and says, 'Let's hear the next one, Jim.' I started playing the next one, and in the middle of it he leans over and says, 'Jim, stop the tape.' Then he turned around and said to the producer, 'Man, that ain't no Bo Diddley tracks. I'm not singing on those tracks.' Then he gets up and storms out of the studio. The producer was shocked. Here we were with seven or eight very expensive tracks—and no Bo. He never did sing on them.

"Our film company found out about the Bo situation and called me to ask if Bo was still in town. I said probably, because he had planned on being here a couple of days. They asked if I would call and make him an offer to come in and cut a Rainier beer commercial. It would be just him and his guitar, and he'd get paid five thousand dollars.

"I called Bo at the hotel and explained what we wanted. He agreed, so I set the room with a vocal mic and guitar amp. He came in and we explained what we wanted: just him singing 'Bo Diddley, Bo Diddley loves Rainier' with a Bo Diddley groove. He did no more than three takes, and it was done. It took maybe an hour. But I'll never forget that look he gave me through those big glasses when he said, 'Stop the tape.'"

000

Michael Botts, formerly from the band Bread, also came to Seattle to record. Gaines remembers him well. "Michael, like me, was a jokester. I set up his drums to get certain sounds, because he had a very unusual setup. He taped up all the heads on the tom-toms so they would get a dead sound; that was his signature sound. But he loved to mess with engineers. So when we were testing sounds, it appeared as if there was a delay on his snare. I was thinking that I must have set it up by mistake on the console. I kept trying to find out where it was coming from, and he kept insisting that I fix whatever's going on. I'm at my wits' end looking faor it, when suddenly he starts laughing his ass off. He could play that snare exactly like there was a delay. He said, 'Jim, I do it to everyone to see how they react.' Damn him! But he sure could play."

Gaines also has fond memories of another spectacular drummer, the afore-mentioned Hal Blaine. At the time, he was one of the most recorded drum-mers in the world and one of the top session players in LA. "I was a little nervous about doing this session with him, because I was told that he was very picky about his drum sound," Gaines remembers. "We were using our in-house drum kits and not his drums. However, he was a very nice guy and a real pro. So I had everything set for him and then we started to test the drum sounds. He played a little, stopped, and asked if I needed any more to set the levels. I told him to listen and see what he thought. When he came in to listen, I was a bit nervous, and then he told me he needed to fix something. He went out and retuned the snare and told me everything was fixed. That's all it took. Thank the Lord!"

Working with reputable and capable musicians was one of the things that kept Jim Gaines's life interesting and his work fulfilling. That meant that he was always on the alert for new opportunities to collaborate with important or interesting talent. But, as he would soon be reminded, not everyone who pres-ents a memorable first impression has what it takes to deliver the real goods.

CHAPTER 8

Sleepless in Seattle

1974–1975

BY THIS POINT IN HIS CAREER, when the phone rang in Jim Gaines's studio, there was every possibility that the caller could be a well-known performer inquiring about Jim's services with a recording. He had acquired a reputation as a producer who could get the sound the artists wanted, and that led to more such opportunities. Still, Jim never knew what the next phone call might bring.

"One night in the middle of a session, I was buzzed by the night receptionist at the studio saying that I had a call," Gaines says. "It was supposedly from Michael Murphey, the singer-songwriter behind such songs as 'Wildfire,' 'Geronimo's Cadillac,' 'What's Forever For?,' and 'Carolina in the Pines.' So naturally I take the call. The person at the other end of the phone asked me if he could come down and look at the studio with the possibility of working there. I told him sure, that I'd stop my session and show him around.

"The receptionist called back a little later and said there was a limo pulling up. I stopped my session and went out to meet him. He came in with a lady friend, introduced himself, and I proceed to quickly show him around. When we were finished with the tour, he said he would call back the next day and reserve some time.

"The next day I get this call from the police asking if I knew or had met a person that I didn't recognize. They told me, 'He goes under the name Michael Murphey.' Oh no. I'm thinking I've been duped, and I'm nervous about exactly who I've been showing around my studio. The police officer then told me that the person in question had escaped from a mental facility, then stayed with a friend from whom he had stolen some money. Now he was out on the town, impersonating the performer Michael Murphey.

"You never know who's calling . . . but it's best to avoid the imposters."

o   In the early 1980s, video transformed the music business. MTV took off like wildfire, adding to the music business model the importance of creating visual imagery to go along with the songs. If you had a song that you wanted to be a hit, you needed a great video to go along with it. Gaines remembers that era well, including the time leading up to it.

"We had a video wing of the company that did Rainier beer ads," he recalls. Rainier beer was, at the time, a popular brand in the Pacific Northwest that was brewed in Seattle, though the company is no longer locally owned. "At the time, the ads showed rows and rows of dominoes falling down in succession. It was kind of cool," Gaines says, "so we decided to do a Rainier Washington version. The director came into the session I was working on at the time and said he was looking for the right 'finger' to start the string of dominoes. He looked at everyone in the room and decided I had the perfect finger. However, first I had to 'audition' by flicking a domino as a test. So they set up some dominoes and filmed my 'audition.' I failed every time I tried, sending the damn thing flying across the room. So much for my video career."

Of course, Gaines had his hands full, being highly in demand for the music recording side of the business. And indeed, it was at about this time that another major opportunity came his way, fortunately involving neither video nor a would-be rock star using an assumed name.

Gaines was finishing up a project with the soul band the Spinners when he received a call from rocker Steve Miller, phoning from Capitol Studios in Los Angeles, where he was finishing up an album. He asked Gaines whether he had any time available to work with him on getting the record finished. He told Gaines that he didn't like working at Capitol Studios for a number of different reasons and he needed to leave.

"I really hadn't worked with Steve, but I had helped out on a project he was involved with and overseeing," Gaines remembers. "It was a solo album by Tim Davis [Miller's former drummer]. I helped them out on the first day by getting them set up and prepped until producer Glyn Johns could arrive and record the album. In short, we somewhat knew each other without really having worked together.

"Anyway, I told him that I was finishing a project and I would be free in four or five days. He agreed and said he would come up with his tapes. He showed up with his driver at the appointed time, tapes in hand. Steve already had a setup to record at his house, and he told me he could do some of the work there rather than going to a studio. At that point, part of the album had already been recorded at CBS Studios in San Francisco and part had been done at his house.

"Most of what Miller wanted me for was to finish a few overdubs and do the mix. We got started on the overdubs first. They consisted of a few vocals and some guitar parts, but mostly it involved some new parts that would segue from the end of certain songs into the songs that followed. To do that, we were using a small, early Casio synthesizer keyboard with built-in sounds such as wind instruments, oboe, and various effects. Steve wanted to capture a kind of spacey feel for the album."

Gaines had a reputation for being a bit of a renegade and using unconventional techniques from time to time, and he notes that some memorable situations emerged from this session. "I asked Steve if he would like to do some vocals from the control room, which he had done at home. Naturally, he said yes. Apparently no one had ever suggested it at any of his other sessions.

"So I set up a basic, small mic that the TV people would use for live broadcasts, because the purpose of those mics was to cut down room leakage [unwanted background sound captured by the microphone]. I had him sit next to me in the control room, and I set up the console so that he could control his headphone mix himself, with reverb and delays."

It didn't take long for Gaines's nonstandard setup to attract unwanted attention. "There we were doing vocals, when my chief engineer came in and proceeded to tell me that we couldn't do the vocals in the control room. He was a straight tech guy, but I went right back at him, asking why it wouldn't work. 'What if the phone rings?' he replies. So I went to the phone, gave it a yank, and handed it to him. Problem solved! Then he asked about the tape machine noise. So I grabbed a blanket and threw it over the machine. Done."

While recording the guitars for the Miller album, Gaines placed the amp under the console at his feet. "Apparently that was another no-no. My chief engineer came in again and chastised me for that."

Later, in May 1976, after that record, *Fly Like an Eagle*, sold five million copies and went to number 2 on the charts, Gaines reports telling the engineer, "Tell me again that I can't do vocals and guitars in the control room."

"Sadly, we never made it to number one, because Fleetwood Mac's *Rumours* had taken the top spot. When they finally relinquished that spot, Stevie Wonder's *Songs in the Key of Life* took its place at number one. We made it as far as number four, then number three and finally number two for quite a while, but never got to number one."

During the process, Gaines discovered the importance of a little luck, along with having a great artist in the studio and the right conditions for producing a hit album. "I was mixing the song 'Fly Like an Eagle' when I realized that I needed more tape at the end of the song so I could capture the wind sound segue into the next track. I went to the shop and got some tape on a reel that was normally used to set up the tape machines. These tapes had some one-kilohertz test tones on them that we used to get them aligned with the machine. We also had this thing called a bulk eraser, a big flat box with a magnet that would clean any previously recorded material off the tape. So I quickly threw the tape on the eraser, swirled it around some, and brought it back to the control room.

"I spooled out about twenty seconds' worth of tape onto the floor and spliced it on. As I was recording more wind noise, I noticed that there were some test tones that were partially left on the tape, and they were somehow in time with the track. When I pulled up the fader and heard that, I thought it could fit perfectly with the song if I could make a deep-space, sonar kind of sound. I ran it into two echo chambers and added some Echoplex delays."

According to Gaines, Miller was half asleep on a sofa in the control room while Gaines was creating these improvised sound effects. "He suddenly wakes up and asks, 'What the hell is that?' I explained what had happened, and he was amazed. That's how the ending of 'Fly Like an Eagle' came about."

Gaines also recalls that the hit song "Rock'n Me" was almost left off the record. "Steve had tried to do the song on several of his previous recordings. Even when I finished mixing, he wasn't sure if he wanted to include it. I asked him to let me try a few edits. I took one chorus that I liked and made a few copies of it and then spliced them in to replace what we had. It worked. I'm not saying it took a genius to figure it out, but it did help." In fact, "Rock'n Me" reached the top spot on the *Billboard* Hot 100 chart and was also a number 1 hit in Canada.

This period also marked the somewhat brief popularity of quadraphonic recording, basically a doubling of the two-channel stereo format. "The studio was set up for it, even though we did very few quad sessions. Capitol wanted a quad mix along with the stereo mix. We had these joystick panning knobs that allow you to control the placement of the tracks. Steve wasn't especially into it, so we decided that we would give them something, but that it would be too far out for them to use. When we finished a stereo mix, I did a quad mix, and just to mess with everybody, I would take the guitar track and spin it around the room. They loved it. We couldn't believe it!

"Making that record was such fun, because we got to step out of the normal routine and play around with it. When we finished, I told Steve, 'Man, this is going to hit big! He said he wasn't so sure. I suggested that we bet on it. If I won I wanted a new pink Cadillac, just like the one Elvis owned. He agreed. Later, when the record was going up the charts, I was in Canada working and I got a call from him telling me, 'Well, you're up to a Ford Pinto. The record just went gold!'" Gaines recalls that though he never got the pink Caddy, he did get a nice bonus.

While Gaines was with Kaye-Smith, Steve Miller brought blues artist James Cotton and his band up to cut some tracks. "When I first heard of Steve, he was performing and recording under the name Steve Miller Blues Band," Gaines recalls. "Boz Scaggs, a friend from high school days in Dallas, was in his band at one time. Steve and Boz had gone to college in Madison, Wisconsin, and on the weekends, Steve would go to Chicago to hang out and play with some of the great blues artists there."

Gaines rightly notes that much of Miller's music was blues based early on. Also, the great guitarist and innovator Les Paul, a friend of Miller's father and Steve's godfather, used to visit him in Dallas and give him guitar lessons.

"Not surprisingly, Steve loved James Cotton. We also brought James to Steve's studio in Oregon and recorded him there later on. Steve was anxious to get him a record deal, but that never worked out."

Before Gaines left Seattle, he began work on the album that would become one of Miller's biggest success stories, *Book of Dreams.* "We experimented with some different grooves," Gaines says. "One day we took some Jimmy Reed grooves, changed the tempos, and even ran them backwards to try for some new sounds." Reed was another influential blues guitarist and singer Miller admired. "But that approach didn't really work out. Regardless, we ended up getting a good start on the album and then eventually recorded quite a bit of it at the Record Plant."

Gaines and Miller would eventually become good friends, and Gaines would have additional opportunities to work full time with Miller in the future.

Gaines and his wife separated while he was working in Seattle. It was a difficult time for Gaines, both personally and professionally; the two of them had practically grown up together and they hung on to the relationship as long as they could. But the demands of Gaines's job proved to be an obstacle the couple could not overcome.

"After the split, I started getting calls to return to Heider's in San Francisco," Gaines says. "They had changed management, and some of the old clients were asking about me. Giving up a job with steady money and going back to a position that really has no guarantees isn't easy. But something told me that I needed to go back. So back to Heider's it was." Gaines was headed back to San Francisco and Wally Heider Studios.

CHAPTER 9

Hightailing It Back to Heider's

1975–1976

ALTHOUGH GAINES HAD HAD plenty of good experiences in his previous work at Heider's studio, he had some second thoughts about his reasons for returning. "To tell you the truth, I'm still not sure why I made the choice to return to work for Heider's in San Francisco, but at the time it seemed to be the right thing to do," Gaines says. "Wally had left the company and I thought at the time that the new management believed that they needed to reestablish some old clients."

One of the first projects Gaines was assigned after his return was for a harmonica player named Norton Buffalo, Steve Miller's background singer and harmonica and tambourine player for Miller's live performances. "He was the best harp player I've ever worked with," Gaines insists. "He also had a great, crooner kind of voice. Steve had gotten him a deal with Capitol Records, and as a result he was designated the executive producer. Norton's music was a hippie-country style kind of thing, and we had a great time doing this record. As a result, we became friends for life." Indeed, Gaines ended up doing two records with Buffalo over the course of the next few years.

000

Other projects followed in rapid succession. Jefferson Airplane had started a label of their own, which they dubbed Grunt Records. They had signed a variety of different artists, recording them at Heider's. Gaines was at least partially involved with several of those efforts.

"I remember one involved flutes and ocean sounds," he recalls. "I have to say, that's not a very dynamic music style for a rock engineer."

Gaines also worked with singer and bassist Larry Graham on some tracks intended for the *Merv Griffin* television show. At the time it was acceptable to sing and play to a prerecorded track. "He came in and set up, with this large pedal board for his bass. We got started on the track, and he kicked in for a bass solo. The power in the studio dropped low enough to stop the tape machine. I said to him, 'What the heck did you do?'

"'I just turned my pedal board on,' he replied. We had to disconnect some things in order to continue. Then, when he came into the room, I noticed his thumb was bleeding; that's how hard he played. Later on, I got to work with him again, first on his own album at the Record Plant, and later when he guested with a Spanish artist at some sessions in Memphis. He is still the best bass player I've ever worked with."

000

At that same time, Sly Stone was working at the Jefferson Airplane studio with some CBS engineers. "Those were some crazy sessions," Gaines reflects. "For starters, he wouldn't let my assistant, who was a woman, walk behind him in the control room." When asked why, Gaines can only shrug. "Who knows? I was filling out some paperwork after my session late one night when I see his driver and bodyguard walking out the door with these big, box-looking things, which I thought were tape boxes. With the next trip he made, I saw that he was carrying out another stack. They turned out to be the acoustic tiles that were supposed to be lining the walls of that room. So I called my boss and told him they were stealing the tiles that were meant to be in that room."

Gaines's superior assured him that he shouldn't worry; Stone's record company would be charged for the tiles. "And they were," Gaines says. "I found out later that Sly was building his own home studio and wanted to use our tiles."

Sly had a special room built next to the new studio they had designed for him at the Record Plant, a combined studio and control room. A sunken console in the middle of the room separated the two sections of the studio, making it possible for the musicians to be situated around the console with no separation between them.

The additional room was an adjoining bedroom with an unusual feature: a bed rigged so that nitrous oxide ("laughing gas") tanks could be placed behind the bed. Tubes ran from the tanks to the top of the bed. Gaines says he is reluctant to speculate on the purpose of this modification.

Although these rooms were built specifically for Stone, according to Gaines, he did very little work there. However, other people certainly made use of the setup, he says.

000

Gaines also had the privilege of working with blues legend John Lee Hooker. "He had a great band with him, including Neal Schon of Journey," Gaines remembers. Schon was a guitarist for Carlos Santana's early recordings, before forming Journey in 1973 with Gregg Rolie.

"In order to get John Lee to do his vocals while we were tracking, we had to get a roadie to whisper the lyrics he'd be singing next, into his ear. I didn't know why he wanted this particular arrangement, and I never found out."

Gaines also had the opportunity to work with Hooker several years later. "This time, we were set up and recording a Santana project at the Record Plant studio. The producer, Roy Rogers, called Carlos and asked if he and I would like to participate with John on a project they were doing. Roy was also trying to get John Lee a record deal. We all said yes. Since we were already tracking, we brought him in and added him to Carlos's band as part of our setup. We all donated our time to help out.

"The track was called 'The Healer' and John Lee did great," Gaines says. "He and Carlos were very good friends, and as a result, anything we could do to help him out, we were happy to do. That record ended up having a bunch of great guest artists on it, and our track turned out to be the title track of the album." In fact, *The Healer*, which included guest performances by artists like Santana, Bonnie Raitt, and Charlie Musselwhite, went gold in the United Kingdom upon its release in 1989 and won a Grammy for Best Traditional Blues Performance.

000

A short time later, Gaines was assigned to work with a young organ player named Michael Perlitch who had been signed to Atlantic. His producer, Geoffrey Hallam, had been involved with several notable British bands, but this particular session, as Gaines reports, was more of a solo project; no band was involved.

"We started out just with organ. He had a Hammond B3 with two Leslie speakers. We had him play the song by himself and later we added some percussion to the tracks.

"Before we rolled tape, he laid out about five joints on the organ and started smoking them, one by one. After he smoked the first one, I asked if he was ready to go, but he said, 'No, I'm not out there yet.'

"We waited until he smoked one or two more. Finally he says, 'I'm ready.' Sure enough, when he started playing, it was like he took us into space with him. It was amazing; I've never heard anyone play like that. We ended up working almost three days nonstop to get the album finished, but what an adventure it turned out to be."

Gaines ventured into a few jazz projects as well. For one of them, he decided to try a new technique for miking the snare drum. "It's something you could only do on a softer style of music," he explains. "I got this drum sound going, and the snare was really big sounding. It just so happened that Herbie Hancock was involved for a track or two, and as a result, he got to hear my new drum sound. He told me that he wanted to play it for David Rubinson at the Automatt." Rubinson, also a prolific producer, worked with artists as diverse as Moby Grape, Hancock, the Pointer Sisters, and Taj Mahal. "A short time later, I got this call from David, telling me that he loved the sound and wanted me to come to his place and duplicate that sound for him. I told him I couldn't leave where I was, but that we could talk later. Eventually I ended up working for or with him."

Gaines was also booked on a Buddy Miles session for four days. "I went in and set up the studio for the first day, but no one showed up. The next day I set up again and ended up shooting pool across the street all day while I was waiting. On the third day, I had the studio call the record company and see what was going on. They said, 'Buddy decided not to come.' That was just the first of many Buddy Miles episodes I would be involved with over the years."

000

Gaines recalls getting a phone call from Steve Miller sometime after he had worked with the artist on *Fly Like an Eagle* and *Book of Dreams*. "One day I got a call from Steve, telling me that he feels like there was something wrong with the mixes that came from the front of the house at his live shows. He asked if I could come to his show at the Oakland Coliseum and simply observe and listen. 'Sure,' I said."

When Gaines arrived at the concert, Miller's manager placed him directly behind the mixing board, near the front of the house. "I was watching the show, and I noticed that the engineer wasn't paying much attention to what was going on with the show—wasn't riding any levels for anyone. Instead, he was really focused on a young girl nearby who was scantily clad as well as the bottle of liquor he had next to him."

After the show the manager came to the mixing board and introduced Gaines as Steve Miller's studio engineer. "You should have seen the look on that guy's face. He realized I had been there the whole time and that I was probably there for a reason."

After the show, Gaines went backstage to see Steve Miller. "Naturally, he asked me what I thought. I told him it would be nice to have someone out front that cared more about the show than getting laid. He then asked me if I would consider coming out and mixing the rest of the tour. I replied that I wasn't really a road guy, and that I wasn't interested in hauling gear and doing the setup. But if he just wanted me to mix, I could try to help out." Miller assured Gaines that he would get the same consideration as the band members if he would only give it a try.

"I ended up helping him finish the tour. I will say this: when studio guys go out to work with PA companies [providing the sound equipment for live concerts], those people generally hate us. They go out of their way to not help us out. The fact is, they're very protective of their jobs. Most of them are great at what they do, but a lot of them don't want studio people there."

On the other hand, Steve Miller certainly wanted Gaines there, so that was that.

000

Gaines recalls other projects from this period that were especially interesting and enjoyable, including the Whispers and the late Texas musician Doug Sahm, formerly of the Sir Douglas Quintet. Sahm is often regarded as one of the icons of Texas music, especially considering the astounding breadth of style displayed in his output: everything from the early rock and roll hit "She's about a Mover" to his heavily conjunto-influenced recordings with Freddy Fender and Flaco Jiménez.

"Doug was especially a lot of fun. He was very talented. That Tejano style was new to me at the time. I remember one session where he was playing all the instruments. First he put down a drum track, then he would start playing piano, and right in the middle of the song, he jumped over to guitar. He was always a little hyper, but we always got our work done. I worked on a couple of records with him."

But soon, Gaines would receive another summons: one that would lead to the next significant period of his career. The success and expertise he had displayed in his work with Steve Miller loomed large in the mind of the artist, as Gaines would learn, and Miller wanted to capitalize on all that Jim Gaines had to offer.

CHAPTER 10

Making Music with Miller

1976–1978

GAINES WAS BECOMING ACCUSTOMED to his producing skills being in demand by this point, and one artist in particular demanded him more than most: Steve Miller. After being on the road with Miller, Gaines received a call from him a few months later in which he learned that Miller had bought a ranch and planned to build a studio there. He wanted to know whether Gaines was interested in a permanent position, which would involve building the studio, doing the engineering, and continuing to do some live mixing. To Gaines, it sounded very interesting.

Steve Miller purchased a 420-acre ranch outside Grants Pass, Oregon, in a beautiful mountain setting. He had built a large building on the property that looked like a modern barn, but he had set aside half the interior space for a studio and the other half as an open area the band could use for rehearsal space, including a full stage setup. The building also housed the band's touring gear, and a few bedrooms were provided for the crew to stay in when they were needed. Miller also had a room for photography, which included a darkroom and a photo shop setup that allowed Miller to indulge his fascination with photography.

There was also a room specifically for making jewelry. This was the era when silver and turquoise jewelry were in vogue, and Gaines says that one of the master carpenters that Miller brought in from Dallas was great at making jewelry. "He taught everyone how to make rings and bracelets, and I still have some of those," Gaines says now.

When Gaines got there, he helped the construction crew with the building as much as he could. "We were getting in studio gear and finishing the structure at the same time," he recalls. "It took a few months to get the studio to the point where we were able to record band tracks. In the meantime, while Steve was touring, we set up a small truck with remote recording gear so we could go out and record some of the shows. However, we found that there were certain cities that weren't worth trying to record in: towns with heavy union influences that would want us to pay a very high fee to record in those venues. It wasn't worth the cost, so we would pass on them."

Gaines would also go out with the band and mix the European shows whenever it proved feasible. "We had some interesting experiences," Gaines relates. "On one particular tour, we were going to do this big show that would be televised live in over ten countries. The theme of the show was kind of a circus opening, with a ringmaster and a live tiger at the beginning. We started rehearsals in London at a big theater, and since we were going to broadcast in these different languages for the show, we wanted to open the show with a greeting in the various native languages. I wanted to record the opening lines with different people announcing in very excited voices, just like a ringmaster would. So I called a school that taught different languages and requested a person from each country to come in and record an opening for us."

Gaines recalls that all was going well, and the various "ringmasters" were getting into the spirit of the thing. "That is, until I got to the guy from Finland. When he was reading the lines, he was very straight and stiff. So I said to him, 'Excuse me, but I really want this to be exciting and joyous.' Then he said to me, 'Mr. Gaines, this is as exciting as it gets in Finland.'"

The opening of the show was supposed to resemble a spectacle reminiscent of a David Copperfield show: a huge Siberian tiger in a cage was supposed to disappear, and Steve Miller would appear in the cage in its place. Gaines says, "I don't know whose idea this was, but it was tricky.

"After the different greetings, the ringmaster would announce the opening of the show. Then the magician, his helpers, and the cage with this beautiful, big tiger would take the stage. The idea was to spin the cage and show the tiger, and then cover it up and spin it again. Then the cover would be removed, and Steve would be in the cage in place of the tiger.

"The secret was that there was a compartment in the floor for Steve to get into, and a wall in the middle of the cage that made it look like the back of the cage itself. The idea was for Steve to get into the floor compartment and then make his way to the back of the cage while it was still spinning.

"The problem was that the tiger was really still in there. Unfortunately, when they were spinning the cage, the weight of the tiger was more than they expected, which made the door jam a little bit, and that made it difficult for Steve to get out. He started yelling at the handlers that he couldn't get out, and finally, after several more spins, he managed to get out."

Gaines says that though Miller eventually managed to get out of the cage, there were some tense moments. "All this was taking place on live television. I can't think of many people who would want to be right beside a five-hundred-pound tiger in a small cage.

"We had another problem in Europe, as well. Over there, their electrical current is powered at 220 volts, and here in the States, we use 110. When you tour with American amps and keyboards, you need a converter for everything to work correctly, and even that doesn't always work the way it should. In the middle of the show, the amps started acting up, and the keyboards began changing settings in midsong. It all kinda went off okay, but we were glad to get out of there."

Happily, things settled down once Gaines got back home. "When we finally got the studio up and running, we would bring the band in to cut tracks, a lot of which came out on later album releases. We also brought in James Cotton, because Steve was working on getting him a deal. We did a lot of experimenting with different styles on the tracks. We also tried working with Cotton's brother Jimmy to get some of his songs recorded and cut some demos with him as well.

000

Miller and his wife were horse enthusiasts, Gaines remembers, and they spent a good deal of time on rides around the ranch and the nearby environs. "They owned some beautiful animals," Gaines recalls. "As a gift, Capitol Records gave Steve a retired Lipizzaner stallion, from the famous riding school in Vienna, Austria. It was gorgeous, and of course it was very well trained."

Gaines even got to do a little ranching work, he says, especially at branding time, when Miller would bring in working cowboys from eastern Washington. "It was a lot of work, but watching the cowboys and their horses work together was amazing. At the end of the day, there would be a big barbecue and a tractor and trailer with hay on it that they would drive around the area while singing and playing acoustic guitar. It was a lot of fun."

Unfortunately, there were some setbacks as well. Someone—apparently not a music fan—went to the local planning commission and complained that Miller wasn't allowed to have a working studio on the ranch. They argued that the area was zoned only for agriculture. "There we were, in the middle of a four-hundred-acre ranch, and we can't record," Gaines said. "It was a battle for Steve that never really went away."

But other problems came into play as well. "Steve and his wife separated towards the end of my time there in Oregon, which made it more difficult for him to get his head into recording," Gaines explains. "I felt like I was a burden on him because I was getting paid but not really accomplishing anything." Gaines knew it was time to move on, once again.

CHAPTER 11

Arriving at the Automatt

1979

GAINES'S NEXT MOVE would bring him to San Francisco, and at that moment, the prospects were promising. "While I was still working for Steve Miller, David Rubinson had called me a couple of times about possibly working with him at the Automatt in San Francisco," Gaines recalls. "He had taken over the old CBS Studios where he had produced several albums. When CBS left, he acquired the studio and refurbished it with more modern equipment. As a result, it was a beautiful place to record."

When Gaines realized Miller's situation was changing, he followed up on Rubinson's contacts, inquiring whether he would be interested in having Gaines come back to San Francisco. "I asked if he was still interested in having me work with him there. His reply was, 'Let's do it!' I told Steve that I thought it would be best if I made the change. He ended up putting the ranch studio on hold and eventually moved to Seattle."

By now, Gaines was a single father with two daughters. "I knew I would really miss living out in the mountains, where I had begun panning for gold with my daughters and teaching them to drive my old truck, even though they were only thirteen and fourteen years old. I loved watching them ride their horses and being country girls." Being a single dad with two teenage girls wasn't easy, Gaines says. "I guess it was kind of a test from God, but we survived." Realizing that things would be different in the busy urban atmosphere of San Francisco, Gaines still felt the move was necessary.

David Rubinson was a highly respected producer with deep connections, and his studio did quite well. He had signed some terrific writers and some excellent artists as well. Gaines also recalls that the equipment Rubinson had installed was some of the most modern in the city. Indeed, the early-mix automation system at the Automatt was a main calling card.

The artists who came to record at the Automatt especially impressed Gaines. He recalls one in particular, Randy Hanson, whom he describes as a "Jimi Hendrix impersonator."

"When he got dressed up as Hendrix, he sort of looked like him," Gaines recalls. "I had seen him a couple of times live, and of course his show was a rock-and-tricks kind of performance. Unfortunately, the writers who were putting together the songs for his album had more experience with R&B and disco material, which I didn't think worked for him. So there were some conflicts between us on the styles we were focusing on."

When the Hanson album was completed and turned in to the label, the record company didn't know what to do with it, Gaines says. "As a result, it never took off. It's too bad, too, because Randy was a terrific guitar player and a pretty good singer."

Gaines also worked with Pearl Harbor and the Explosions, the first production for David Kahne's new label, 415 Records. Kahne had started his career as a musician and eventually became director of artists and repertoire for 415, a seminal punk and New Wave label based in a tiny office upstairs at the Automatt. Kahne had discovered Pearl Harbor, cut some demos with them, and secured them a deal.

"David was experimenting with different sounds and ways to approach the recording," Gaines says. "As a result, we were doing some nonconventional recording techniques. He had done some engineering as well, so he knew what he was looking for." These were the early days of raw, grungy music styles, Gaines notes. Even though the record didn't sell that well, the label was impressed with his and Kahne's work.

"David eventually ended up in LA, where he became a major producer for several big acts. I'm very proud of him and happy that we had the opportunity to work together."

Gaines also had the opportunity to work with some exceptional young engineers. Leslie Ann Jones, the daughter of 1940s musician and bandleader Spike Jones, was one of them. She later went on to be an important staff member at the National Academy of Recording Arts and Sciences

(NARAS). Later, she ran the George Lucas studios. "She was a great engineer," Gaines says.

Fred Catero was Rubinson's main engineer at the Automatt, and before that, he had been with CBS as well. At that time, he was considered one of the top engineers in the city. "He taught all of us a few tricks," Gaines remembers. "I'm glad I got to work with him and learn from him."

Gaines also recalls the time Commander Cody and His Lost Planet Airmen came in to record. "George Frayne, who was the leader of the band, was aiming to be more of a solo artist. The band had a big hit in 1972 with 'Hot Rod Lincoln,' but I think the record company wanted him to have a softer country-rock style, more like the Eagles." Cody, however, was noted for his raw, rockabilly style that borrowed more from the truck stop than the concert stage. "One of the songs I recorded for him was 'Two Triple Cheese, Side Order of Fries,' and that one got a lot of airplay." Subsequently, the multitalented Cody would produce a video by the same name that is on permanent exhibit at the New York Museum of Modern Art.

"The Bay Area really seemed to attract this style of music. There were quite a few similar-sounding bands around, doing records of that sort. Working with George was fun because he was always upbeat. He was also a painter, and he has a couple of books featuring his work. To tell you the truth, I'm not an art critic, but to me, his painting looked like paint by numbers. I even asked him, 'George, are you sure this isn't paint by numbers?' He just laughed."

During his time at the Automatt, Gaines did some demos for a few artists that eventually ended up getting record deals. Unfortunately, he didn't get to record the actual albums. One of those was Tommy Tutone, a band that later had the hit "867-5309/Jenny." Gaines didn't get to work on the project, however; it was recorded in Los Angeles with another producer and engineer.

"There were three of those projects, almost back to back," Gaines says. "The last of them was Huey Lewis and the News. As we were finishing Huey's demos, the record company A&R guy, who was sitting right beside me in the control room, said to me, 'I want to sign this band, so we'll do the record right here with Gaines.' But a month or two later they were in LA, recording with someone else. That particular record came out and did nothing, because they had changed the band's sound, made it way too slick." Gaines recalls that the Lewis band was more of a fun, raw, live-sounding act, which was reflected in the demos he produced at the Automatt.

"It was disappointing. After the Huey Lewis project went away, I sat down and asked myself, 'What the hell is going on here?' I've never played politics and I never will, so I couldn't compete with the LA version of the game. I said, 'To hell with this,' and I decided I was just going to leave the business. Here I was with all these hits to my credit, and I still couldn't compete.

"I decided I'd pull out, go back to Oregon, and do something else for a living. So I drove up one weekend, found a house, came back, and told David, 'I can't deal with those situations anymore.' He was very disappointed. David had treated me well, and I still appreciate all that he did for me."

Nevertheless, Gaines had made up his mind. He was returning to the country life in Grants Pass, Oregon.

CHAPTER 12

Return to Grants Pass

1979–1980

MUSIC WASN'T ON JIM GAINES'S MIND when he made his move back to Grants Pass. Taking care of his family was his foremost priority, and at this point he was about fed up with the recording industry.

"I had no idea what I was going to do," he now says, looking back on that time. "I was looking around for employment ideas. One thought was to work for the local radio station. As I was interviewing with the station manager, he looked at me and said simply, 'You're overqualified, and you'll eventually go back to recording.' I interviewed with an insurance company and they told me the same thing. There was a small studio in the area that did a gospel radio show as well as some recording, so I ended up doing a little work there."

However, Gaines had decided that he would be better off buying a business or starting something new. Initially, he was hoping to find an opportunity that would allow him to work, but still take off for a few days if a recording session became a possibility. "However, Steve [Miller] had left Oregon by this time, so there wasn't any work there. I eventually ended up buying a windshield repair franchise. It was a new kind of business that was getting started in various parts of the country, and I ended up buying the rights to operate in two counties in my area."

Gaines says that among his bread-and-butter accounts were used car lots. He also sought out specialized businesses like sheriff's departments, highway patrol offices, gravel trucking companies, and the like. "But my biggest client," he says, "was the Bureau of Land Management. BLM trucks ran all over the mountain roads, which happened to be mostly gravel." Naturally, that led to lots of cracked and chipped windshields.

"When I first started going into the garages and auto shops to talk to their managers, they wouldn't have anything to do with me at first, because I was nicely dressed and I looked like a salesman," Gaines says. "I was sitting at home one night, trying to figure out what I needed to do to get to these guys to talk to me, and I came up with the idea of buying a used mechanic's smock with grease stains on it. It even had the name 'Harold' imprinted on it. So I put it on and then went back to the same people, and they now thought it was okay to talk to me. That smock turned my whole business around." Gaines had remarried by this time, and his new wife wanted a business, so he purchased a diet and skin care center for her.

Despite all this, Gaines realized that he couldn't entirely abandon all thoughts of recording. He did a session for a second album by Norton Buffalo, also enjoying the chance to reunite with his old friend.

"We did it on an almond ranch in Modesto, California," Gaines recalls. "We were working sixteen- to eighteen-hour days so we could get it done quickly. We worked so many hours that my ears started ringing." Gaines remembers taking a break from the control board one evening to go out into the orchard for some quiet. "All of a sudden, the irrigation system kicked on, and I got soaking wet before I could get back into the control room." By this time he was wide awake, but this provided another type of wake-up call, as well. "I told myself after that I would never work that many hours again. It scared me to know I could be hurting my ears."

Meanwhile, Gaines found himself traveling between two different worlds: fixing windshields one day, and running out to record sessions another day. One session during this period involved a band from Seattle. Traveling to one of these sessions on a flight with a stop in Portland, Gaines relates that the pilot came on the speaker just as the aircraft was approaching the Portland airport. "He said that there was something he wanted us to see. He opened up the curtains to the cockpit, and there in front of us was Mount Saint Helens as it was erupting."

The mountain was very close to the airport, so after his flight landed, Gaines continued to watch the eruption from the terminal. "My Seattle flight finally took off, and we ended up flying right next to the volcano. In fact, the pilot angled the plane so that we were looking right down on it. It remains one of the most amazing things I have ever seen in my life. I had flown and driven by Mount Saint Helens many times, but here was this giant plume of black and gray smoke pouring out of it; part of the mountaintop was completely gone. All of the huge trees were lying on their sides, looking like a giant's game of pick-up sticks."

The explosion made headlines for days and weeks to come. Gaines had witnessed one of nature's most powerful and destructive phenomena.

000

Gaines's next recording project took him to Canada. He was no stranger to working there. Indeed, in the past, the typical protocol involved him going through Canadian immigration and explaining that he was there to work, telling them where the work would take place and the length of time required. After that, a work permit would be issued.

But this time would be different.

"I flew into Vancouver to do some sessions with a band called Fosterchild," Gaines explains. "When I arrived, I told the immigration officer why I was there. He told me, 'There's a new law, and you have to have a work permit before arriving.'"

To Gaines's consternation, he was then questioned and his personal effects were searched. Then he was placed under arrest, taken to the airline desk, and told that he had to go back to Seattle and get a permit at the Canadian consulate. "They escorted me to the plane, put me in my seat, and stood by the airplane door until we departed. I can only imagine what all the other passengers on the plane thought about me."

The next day, armed with a telefax from CBS Records giving the particulars of the working arrangement for the session, Gaines went to the consulate and finally got his permit. "I flew back to Vancouver, first stopping in Victoria to clear customs and immigration. I handed my paperwork to the agent, and he promptly told me that I was missing a form. He then informed me that I had to return to Seattle. I told him that I had a band and a studio waiting for me, and that if I did go back to Seattle, I would never come back to this country again." The agent reluctantly allowed Gaines to proceed, but the delay had forced the holding of the flight that would take him on to Vancouver. Once again, he says, the looks on the faces of the other passengers said it all: they were not happy.

"I was almost thrown out of Canada a second time, and I haven't been back since."

000

After spending some additional time in Grants Pass, Gaines got a call from Huey Lewis and Bob Brown, the singer's manager. They wanted Gaines to come back to San Francisco and work on Lewis's new album. They told him that they had tried several people to produce the recording, but in the end they decided Gaines was the only one who understood the direction the band was trying to go.

"I told them I felt like I had gotten screwed on the last project, and as a result I didn't know if I wanted to get involved again. But they told me that this time they had the okay to do whatever they wanted. So after a long conversation, I agreed to come back. Huey and Bob are the ones responsible for my Bay Area comeback." Soon, Gaines was back in the studio, working with Huey Lewis and the News to produce their second album, *Picture This.*

CHAPTER 13

Back to the Bay

1980–1981

THE RECORDING OF *PICTURE THIS* took place in several studios, including Gaines's former stomping grounds at the Automatt. The objective was to capture the vibrant sound the band was known for and to make the album feel as live as possible.

"It was fun getting the project up and going," Gaines says. "Also, Huey had this old Mercedes Benz with a cracked windshield, so there I was, fixing it in the parking lot of the hotel," he recalls.

Gaines was happy to be working with the band again. "We tried out some different ideas on the new tracks. Fortunately, this time we had more time to play with the sound. One of the main things we wanted to do was make sure we had the key songs in place. The guys had written some original material, but there were outside songs that we looked at as well."

Gaines points out that at this time, no one had really heard of Huey Lewis and the News. One of the first things that had to be resolved was the band's name. Originally they called themselves Huey Lewis and the American Express. Advisers warned them that there could be legal problems with the American Express corporation, so they changed their moniker to Huey Lewis and the News to avoid any conflict.

"I loved working with lead guitarist Chris Hayes, because he and I were both into trying some different guitar sounds," Gaines remembers. "In addition, the drummer, Bill Gibson, and I worked on some drum sounds that he wanted. The guitarist and saxophone player Johnny Colla was very important in helping with arrangements and vocals. Keyboard player Sean Hopper had some new keyboards and also wanted to try new ideas. And Huey himself is lots of fun to work with. He knows what he wants and he's always very positive and upbeat. All in all, it was a great team."

Gaines says that he and Lewis would go back to Gaines's hotel room at night and listen to the new songs coming in for consideration. Some of these were from Bruce Hornsby, who would later score a top hit with "The Way It Is," backed by his band, The Range. Another was written by Phil Lynott, the leader of Thin Lizzy, whom Lewis had known when he was in England. At this time, Gaines says, Hornsby was playing keyboards for Sheena Easton, the Scottish singer who had a major hit with her song "9 to 5" (later retitled "Morning Train" for the American market). But he was also being signed to Brown and Lewis's publishing company. Some of his songs would be included on *Picture This.*

"We were almost done recording when the producer, Mutt Lange, sent us another song that he had written. Mutt and Huey had become friends when Huey was in England with his old band, Clover, which also included Sean Hopper. Huey was the harp [harmonica] player at the time, and Alex Call was the band's lead singer. The song Mutt sent us was called 'Do You Believe in Love.' We tried to stay true to the demo version because it was so good. The harmonies on that song are very important, and all the guys in Huey's band had great voices that blended really well. Johnny Colla helped put together the background parts."

The last-minute addition to the album would prove fortunate. "Do You Believe in Love" remained on the *Billboard* charts for thirty-five weeks, peaking at number 7. The follow-ups, "Hope You Love Me Like You Say You Do" and "Working for a Living" also became top 40 hits.

"One of the stories I always get asked to tell is about Huey and how we recorded his voice," Gaines says. "Huey didn't want me to put any effects on his voice except some tape delay. After the album was out, there were all these interviews that focused on the making of *Picture This,* so I told all of the interviewers that I had a new piece of gear built for me. I told them it was called the Frigenhimer 451, and it was the secret to Huey's vocal sound. Man, these writers went crazy over that and started searching for one. Huey heard about the story, and so he went along with it. They even had a delay unit at the front of the house [for live concerts] with that label on it, just in case anyone asked. For years, people wanted to know where they could get a Frigenhimer 451. We had a lot of fun putting one over on the tech people."

Gaines mentions that during the *Picture This* sessions, he tried out a new type of digital tape machine. "They were just coming out with it, and the group wanted me to test it. I agreed that I would try it, but I also wanted my normal analog machine going at the same time, for backup. Those were the days when digital was trying to get into the market, and I was told that they would need their tech guy standing by while it was being used. But what they didn't tell me was that it was going to cost us an additional five hundred dollars per day for him to be there. When I heard that, I told them, 'I think not; we'll pass.'"

With *Picture This* climbing the album charts, Gaines felt that he was truly back in the recording business. "It was a great reentry," he says.

While Gaines was finishing the Huey Lewis project, guitarist Ronnie Montrose, learning that Gaines was in town, called to ask about the possibility of working together. He was rerecording his album because he had just lost lead singer Sammy Hagar and wanted to start the process over again.

"Ronnie was at the Automatt," Gaines says. "After meeting with him and his manager Bill Graham, I said yes. Ronnie and I had worked briefly on Van Morrison's album *Saint Dominic's Preview.* I always considered him a great guitar player, a genius in fact. He built a lot of his own gear, including a guitar that had each string going to its own output for a separate amp. The concept is almost impossible, but Ronnie had been working with Galen Kruger to help design a line of amps, which we ended up using. When the sound goes through the speakers with him playing the strings just right, it just waltzes across the stereo spectrum."

Gaines remembers that Montrose also had a great band. "His keyboard player was Mitchell Froom, who went on to become a great producer and record executive." Indeed, Froom would go on to work with a broad array of influential artists, including Los Lobos, Paul McCartney, Elvis Costello, Sheryl Crow, the Bangles, Randy Newman, and many others.

Gaines says that the tracking and overdubs went very quickly. "Ronnie was a positive and fun-loving person all the time," Gaines says in retrospect. "He loved drinking strong coffee, so one night after being on a coffee high, he told me, 'Jim, I can walk up that wall!' I said, 'Show me!' Damned if he didn't get a couple of steps up before coming down. I had never seen anyone do that before."

Davey Pattison, Montrose's new vocalist, was Scottish. Gaines claims he had a great White soul voice, but that he couldn't understand half of what Pattison said in his normal speaking voice. "When he was singing, you could understand everything. But when Pattison talked to me, Ronnie's road crew guy had to interpret for me. Seriously, though, there are a lot of great soul and R&B singers from Scotland, Ireland, and England. It must be in the water . . . or it could be in the Scotch."

The album, titled *Gamma 3*, went to number 72 on the charts and yielded a fairly successful single, "Right the First Time," which went to number 27.

As Gaines was finishing up his work with Montrose, legendary promoter Bill Graham approached him and asked whether he would stay an extra day or two to record Carlos Santana. As Graham explained, they were looking for someone new to work on Santana's upcoming album. Gaines was not only back in the recording business; he was once again in high demand.

CHAPTER 14

Scoring with Santana

1980

THE SANTANA ASSIGNMENT would soon prove to be a perfect segue from the Montrose sessions. In fact, Gaines's association with guitar great Carlos Santana would become one of the most meaningful of his career.

"After the first day of the Santana session, Ray Etzler came to me and said, 'Well, Jim, what are you doing the next six months?' I said, 'I don't know, Ray, what do you want me to do?' He said, 'You are recording Santana's new record.'" The other candidates didn't even get a chance to audition.

Gaines recalls that the Santana sessions weren't particularly frenzied. They weren't required to work every day, and Carlos rarely worked on Sunday, because he kept that day for his family.

"Sometimes we didn't even work on Saturday," Gaines says, "so I would drive home to Oregon for the weekend, which was a five- to six-hour drive." Also, because Santana would go out to do shows, there were frequent breaks in the recording schedule.

"The Santana band is a very powerful-sounding group," Gaines says. "And Carlos is the best guitar player I've ever worked with. The emotion that he puts into his playing is incredible. He is very picky about getting the right sound out of his amps and onto tape."

Gaines believes that one of the reasons he had the opportunity to work with Santana so many times over the years was that he really cared about pleasing the artist and wanted the best guitar sound that he could get for him.

The band setup was very large, Gaines recalls, including three percussionists as well as the rhythm section. The percussion section, of course, with its heavy Latino influence, is a large part of the Santana sound.

"We referred to them as the heart of the rhythm section," Gaines recalls. "He wanted them to be tracked live with the band. While we were working on the album *Shangó*, Gregg Rolie came in to help out on a couple of tracks. Even though he had left the band, along with Neal Schon, to start Journey, he and Carlos remained friends. I believe that by this time he had left Journey. He was only there for a few days to lend a few ideas."

Gaines remembers a discussion about Rolie's experience playing at Woodstock. "I don't think Santana was on the original lineup, but Bill Graham had gotten them to replace someone who couldn't make it," Gaines says. He relates that Rolie's memories included an LSD-induced hallucination in the middle of Santana's set.

Rolie told Gaines, "Some of us had done some acid before going on. In the middle of the show, I looked down at the floor, and it wasn't there; it was just blue sky. I started to freak out, because I felt like I was suspended in the air. I looked over to Carlos to tell him, 'I'm floating,' but I couldn't get the words out. He's looking at me and wondering what's going on."

Nevertheless, they finished the show and received a great response. Woodstock helped propel Santana even further. In 1999, Gaines had the opportunity to accompany Carlos Santana to the thirtieth-anniversary event Woodstock '99.

Gaines remembers a producer named John Ryan being at the Santana sessions for a song or two. "He was an LA guy," Gaines said. "I don't think he had much experience producing. I felt like he had more to do with the song than with the production. The entire time we were working on his songs, he was on the phone, with his cowboy boots propped on the console. When the band would finish a pass on the song, he would look at me and ask what I thought. If I said we should do it again, he would get on the talk-back mic and tell them to do it again. Then he went back to his call.

"He happened to be in the room when we were fixing a bass part on a previously recorded track that he had nothing to do with. So he decided that he should get a partial credit on the song. Later, management came to me and asked what had happened. I told them, and they decided not to give him any part of that song.

"When we had finished his track, he took it with him to LA so he could mix it with the people he worked with there. When he sent me back the mix, he asked me to listen to it before playing it for Carlos. I did, but it was so bright it could rip your head off. Then Carlos came in and asked to hear it, so I played about thirty seconds of it before he turned to me and told me to stop. He told me he never wanted to hear that again. Naturally, John was disappointed."

Alex Ligertwood was Santana's singer at the time. Like Davey Pattison, he was also Scottish. "That boy could really sing," Gaines insists.

Gaines and the group spent several months working on the album, and when it came time to mix, it was decided that Bill Szymczyk, who had previously produced the Eagles, should do the honors. "Bill had a studio in Miami, so we all flew to Florida to attend the mixing sessions," Gaines explains. "He was friendly to me, but I was not allowed in the control room while he was mixing, and neither was Carlos. Only after he finished were we allowed to listen. I thought this was odd, especially excluding Carlos. But that's how Szymczyk worked. There were a couple of tracks that got some chart action, and it was a good album, one of several I got to work on with Carlos."

After segueing from Huey Lewis to Ronnie Montrose and then to Santana, Gaines found himself back in engineering full time, going from one project to another. "I would finish one record and go straight to the next one," he says.

"While working on the Santana album, my wife apparently decided that she wanted to be with another man. I could feel something was wrong, because she would disappear almost every day at the same time. When I came home too early from a trip, I caught her coming in from a weekend stay with this guy. I asked where she had been, and she told me she and a girlfriend had spent the night in Medford after attending a ski swap meet. However, Medford is only twenty miles away, and she didn't ski. So I picked up the phone, called her girlfriend, and asked her if she had she seen my wife. She said she hadn't seen my wife in a couple of weeks. I handed the phone to my wife and said, 'Your alibi just gave you up.' That was the end of that marriage."

Though Gaines tells the story in a somewhat lighthearted way, it was a devastating blow. On the other hand, Gaines now had no reason not to put his full focus on his career. Staying busy was what he needed to do, and a perfect opportunity was about to present itself.

CHAPTER 15

Returning to the Record Plant

1981–1982

JIM GAINES WAS BACK in the Bay Area, and word of his arrival didn't take long to get around. He soon received a call from Terry Delsing, manager of the Record Plant, one of San Francisco's leading studios. Delsing, learning that Gaines had returned to the area and was working on various projects, asked whether they could set up a meeting that involved Gaines using the Record Plant as his base.

In 1981, the studio had been sold to Laurie Necochea, who had received a major legal settlement in a medical malpractice suit. The previous owner, Chris Stone, had decided to sell it to her after the death of his partner, Gary Kellgren. Necochea was a big fan of the Doobie Brothers and also an ardent admirer of other Bay Area bands. Owning the studio allowed her to spend time with some of her favorite musicians.

Steve Malcom and Bob Hodas had helped her negotiate the purchase and stayed on to work at the studio for a short time. The deal specified that the name of the studio be changed simply to "The Plant." She also hired Terry Delsing as the studio manager, and he added several new consoles and upgrades as well as some changes in the acoustics, all for the good, in Gaines's opinion.

"When Terry found out about my recent projects in San Francisco, he told Laurie that they ought to pursue me," Gaines explains. "When I was asked what I thought about it, I told them that if I came, I wanted two things. One, I wanted to be a priority in terms of getting studio time for my projects and to be able to use the studio of my choice. The second thing I needed was a house or condo. I didn't want to sell my house in Oregon at this point, in case I decided to move back." They agreed.

"I moved, happy that I wouldn't have to stay in a hotel anymore," Gaines continues. "One of the first projects I worked on was a group called Pink Cloud, a group from Japan. The studio had a house in Mill Valley for bands to stay in as needed. This particular band brought their family with them to vacation while they were recording."

Pink Cloud was a trio that included a very well-known jazz/rock drummer and bass player. The guitar player and singer was a successful young television star back in Japan. He was also the only member of the group who spoke English.

"I asked them how they came up with the name," Gaines says, "and their response was that it referred to one of the nicknames for LSD or for the trip that resulted after taking it. For them, recording in the Bay Area meant that they were in close proximity to one of the places that actually birthed LSD."

Gaines says that working with a band in which many of the members didn't speak English could be challenging, though he managed, somehow. "While we were working, they would sometimes stop to take a break, and they would say to me, 'Jim-san, we take break now.' Then the entire band would pile into the bathroom at once." Gaines says that the mirror shelves in the restroom offered a convenient surface for chopping and consuming recreational drugs.

"When they came out of the bathroom, the cocaine they had indulged in could be seen in their mustaches, eyebrows, and beards. It was pretty obvious what their break had been for. I asked them if it had been permissible to do drugs in the studios in Japan, and they said, 'Absolutely not.'"

Nevertheless, Gaines remembers Pink Cloud as an enjoyable project with entertaining musicians. He says the album was completed fairly quickly, the group's drug use notwithstanding.

One of the people who had originally been responsible for manufacturing LSD and distributing it to the Bay Area bands in the late sixties was Owsley "The Bear" Stanley. He was still active in the early eighties and would occasionally drop by one of Gaines's sessions.

"He always had some kind of advice for me," Gaines recalls. "Once, Huey

Lewis and I ran into him at LAX while we were waiting for a plane. We asked him where he had been, and he said that he moved to a certain mountain in Australia, because it was going to be one of the few safe places to be when a second holocaust came. Then he proceeded to try and sell us some precious stones he had smuggled back with him. That guy was really something else."

000

Around this same time, Jimmy Barnes, the former singer of the Australian band Cold Chisel, had decided to go solo with a new album. In Gaines's estimation, Barnes had many stylistic similarities with Bruce Springsteen. "His music was hard-rocking, made for the working man, so it was appropriate that his album was called *For the Working Man*," Gaines says.

"Most of the album had been recorded in New York with some top players. My part of the project was to remix two songs for Journey's Jonathan Cain, who had written some of the songs on the album and produced a couple: 'Ride the Night Away' and 'Without Your Love.' One of the tracks he wrote, the title tune 'Working Class Man,' debuted at number one in Australia and would go on to become Jimmy's signature song. It went seven times platinum there as well."

The second album Gaines recorded at the Plant, *Freight Train Heart*, was produced and partially written by Jonathan Cain. The artists on the roster included an all-star rhythm section, including Rod Stewart's drummer Tony Brock, Randy Jackson on bass, Jonathan Cain on keyboards, Jonathan's Journey bandmate Neal Schon on guitar, and Huey Lewis playing harmonica.

"When I was setting up the drum kit," Gaines says, "Tony's drum tech came in and took a look at my setup. I had a drum riser that I had custom made to lift the drums off the floor in order to get more bottom from the kick [bass drum] and toms. He told me, 'Tony's not going to like it.' I suggested that we give it a try, and I said, 'If he isn't happy with it, we will change it.' When he came in and started playing, I recorded it and played it back to him. Fortunately, he loved it. I was relieved I didn't have to break down the riser."

The tracking would produce some great results that included capturing the vocal sound Jimmy Barnes was after. "His voice was roughed up; he had that classic, hard-drinking kind of voice, and we managed to get it sounding just right on the tape. Later, Jimmy and the record company didn't agree on some of the guest solos, so he got the tapes and took them back to Australia to redo some of those parts. He added what he wanted and with whom he wanted, and then he released it."

Apparently, Barnes's judgment was sound; the album debuted at number 1 and eventually went five times platinum back home in Australia. It would soon become one of his better-selling albums. It was later named one of the top 100 rock albums of all time by *Powerplay* magazine.

"I am very glad I got to work on that important project," Gaines says in retrospect. "Jonathan Cain was great to work with, and we would work together again when we recorded Journey."

More Plant Pursuits

1981–1982

WHEN GAINES FIRST ARRIVED back at the Record Plant, Rick James was in the middle of a recording session. What happened next made for an interesting encounter.

"The great engineer Tom Flye was recording him," Gaines recalls. "Rick was living at the studio, and his bedroom was the Boat room, which had a waterbed floor and doubled as the isolation booth. He always had a big group of people with him, and they worked really long hours. Rick himself would roam the halls and visit with everyone when he wasn't working. However, he had this problem: after he showered, he would walk around with nothing on but a towel while he was socializing. When he was talking to our lady staff people, he would 'conveniently' drop the towel.

"Now, women who work in recording studios see a lot of things, and they're typically not shy, but this was too much. So I was asked to say something to him about this. I talked to the person who was his so-called manager, and eventually it stopped."

Gaines says that working at the Record Plant in San Francisco allowed him to live in Marin County and still be close to work without having to go into the city, which he enjoyed. "Sausalito is a beautiful place, and the studio was only a few doors from the bay. It was nice when you had enough break time to walk and see the water."

The studio building had once been a train station, Gaines says, and one of the original partners, Gary Kellgren, had done a great job with the original construction. Seeing young Laurie Necochea, the new owner, come in and visit was a joy for everyone who worked there, Gaines remembers. "We knew she was thrilled to be there, see the artists, and hang out. But we also knew she was going to have a short life ahead of her, given all her medical challenges. Eventually her trust would recommend that she sell the place so that all her money could be devoted to ensuring that she would have the care she needed. Sadly, she passed away a year later."

Gaines remembers that the Record Plant was like a family in many ways. Artists and bands would frequently drop by to see who was recording and visit for a while. At any given time, members of the Doobie Brothers, Journey, Jefferson Starship, Van Morrison, or other artists from nearby Marin would drop by to hang out.

"Tommy Johnston of the Doobies was there a lot," Gaines recalls. "After he had left the band, I helped him do some of his demos. Later I would work with him again when he rejoined the band."

One project Gaines attempted was with a group that called themselves the Bus Boys. "We had worked on a track, but the lead singer wanted to replace the kick [bass] drum part," he says. "We spent six hours trying to do just that, and the drummer finally got burned out from all the attempts. It was a total waste of time. I finally told them that I was leaving, and I let my assistant take over." Gaines says that his departure was timely, since at about that time the lead singer decided to demonstrate his toughness by gulping down a bottle of hot sauce. "At that point it was indeed time for me to leave."

000

Gaines also recalls working with a group called 707. "These guys were one of the reasons Terry Delsing had remodeled the studio," he explains. "They were a Marin-based band that everyone projected would really break out. They were good musicians and they had good vocals, but they could never pull off that much-needed hit single. I remember thinking while working on that project that they needed to do what Huey [Lewis] did: look for songs that came from outside the band. However, they never did."

000

About this time, Gaines connected with producer Bob Johnston, who had been at the studio during its early days. Among his many credits was the production of Bob Dylan's hugely influential *Nashville Skyline* album.

"He lived in Marin and was always running in and out with different projects," Gaines explains. "I got to work on a few of them. He was a very upbeat guy, but he also smoked a lot of pot. I found that generally made for a contrast in a person's attitude and personality. I remember that on several occasions we actually had an official joint roller in the room. The pot smoke would be so thick at times that when I looked up over my head, there would be a blue haze floating a few feet above me. I had to take breaks just to clear my mind. Meanwhile, Bob could be very scattered. We would be in the middle of recording vocals, and he would jump up and say, 'Let's do guitars.' There was always that constant change. But for all that, he was still great to work with."

000

Gaines also recorded with Buddy Miles, who, among other credits, had been the drummer for Jimi Hendrix. Gaines had first met Miles when he was staying in Steve Miller's guest house in San Francisco, while doing the *Book of Dreams* album.

"Buddy lived a few houses down the hill. He occasionally would show up late at night looking for Steve. More often than not, he would be messed up [under the influence of drugs or alcohol]. I would tell him that Steve wasn't there, and eventually he would leave. There was another time when I was working on some Tower of Power sessions, and he would show up and want to play on the record. We would let him do some hand claps or tambourine, just to get him out."

Miles would eventually go to prison for tax evasion and other assorted misdeeds, which resulted in his losing most of his possessions. "One day, I got a call from his manager," Gaines says, "who wanted to talk to me about doing a work release program for him. They would let him out of prison for the day to work, and then he would go back at night.

"I said, 'No way.' I remembered his ego and his demanding attitude. I told Buddy's manager that I didn't need any crazy sessions in my life."

A couple of months later, Gaines says, the manager called again and explained that Miles had undergone "a change" in prison. "Now, I realize that being locked up can change some people, so I agreed to meet with him and have a talk. The day he arrived, he was accompanied by his manager and someone from the prison. When he walked in, he looked broken. He barely looked at me. He said, 'How are you doing, Reverend Gaines?'

"Everyone knows that I never got into drugs, and as a result, I was known as 'Mr. Clean.' But having him call me 'Reverend Gaines' was quite different. I said to him, 'Buddy, the question is, how are you doing?' He said he had been writing some great songs in prison and wanted to have me record them. We talked, and after determining how the program would affect his hours in the studio, I agreed to work with him, but it would have to be on my terms. There would be no bullshit and, of course, no drugs. We would have to completely concentrate on work. The ego had to be checked at the door. I used some really tough language."

Everyone agreed to Gaines's terms. "Buddy said, 'Thank you very much, Reverend.' He would call me that until the day he died."

Gaines remembers that when he was working with Miles, there would be either a social worker or a prison official at the sessions. "The sessions went well, but as we were finishing, Bill Graham booked him a show at the Kabuki Theater [a venue on Post Street in San Francisco that hosted acts like Men at Work, Eddie Money, and Metallica; it is now a cinema]. The afternoon of the sound-check rehearsals, two marshals showed up, arrested him, and took him back to prison. He had failed his drug test."

Ultimately, Miles would serve only a short time, and when he was released, Gaines continued to work with him. "I suggested to Carlos Santana that he might want to give Buddy a guest shot on the sessions we were working on with his band. Bill Graham asked to come in and oversee the vocals. In the process, Bill was actually directing him and showing him how to express emotion. Bill was very theatrical and always quite expressive. He liked to wave his arms about quite a bit. He told Buddy that he wanted him to sound like he was flying, then descending like an angel, eventually landing on a horse that's running along the beach.

"Buddy looked at me and silently mouthed, 'What the hell is he talking about?' I didn't have an answer."

Miles would go on to sit in with Carlos Santana for a few shows, but then, Gaines says, he decided he wanted to play guitar. "Of course, there was only one guitar player in that band, and that was Carlos."

Miles's album never came out, Gaines reports. "It got tangled up in the operation when the Record Plant was taken over by the Feds."

But this would not be the end of Gaines's experiences with Buddy Miles.

CHAPTER 17

Getting the News

1983

HUEY LEWIS AND THE NEWS, whom Gaines had recorded previously at the Automatt, were on the cusp of success when Gaines was assigned to record their next album. He recorded them at both the Record Plant and Fantasy Studios. The reason, he recalls, was that they couldn't get all the time needed at the Record Plant.

Prior to recording, the band's manager, Bob Brown, had separated from his wife and moved in with Gaines. "Huey called the house one morning and said he was anxious to play us a song that had just come in," Gaines recalls. "It was written by Mike Chapman and Nicky Chinn, the songwriting team responsible for a number of hits at that time. The song was called 'Heart and Soul.' Bob listened on the extension, but his comment was that it wasn't soulful enough. However, both Huey and I liked it, so we decided to try and cut it."

They thought the song was unreleased, but once they began tracking it, one of the assistant engineers commented that not only was it out in the world, but he had heard covers of the song by the Bus Boys, Suzi Quatro, and Exile.

Thinking that they had already put in quite a bit of time on the track, Gaines and the artists decided to finish it and put it aside, at least for the time being. Ultimately it would become the band's first single from the *Sports* album.

Meanwhile, Gaines was trying to get used to the different environment at Fantasy Studios. "It was very corporate in look and feel," he recalls. "You had to sign in, go to your room, and not bother any of the other folks who happened to be recording that day. It was totally different from anything I had ever experienced before. On weekends, there were guards to greet you and sign you in. A couple of times Huey and I would be ringing the heck out of the buzzer, but it would take forever for them to let us in. It was not a great situation."

Still, working with Huey Lewis and the News proved to be an interesting experience. "When we were recording the song 'Heart of Rock and Roll,' we needed to simulate the sound of a heartbeat," Gaines says. "First we tried doing it with a kick drum, but it didn't have the sound we were looking for. Of course, how many people even know what a heartbeat really sounds like? I didn't, but I knew we had to find something that everybody at least would think sounded like a heartbeat.

"The keyboard player Sean Hopper and I spent about six hours messing with different sounds. He happened to have a new keyboard that did come close, but I came up with several tricks to get it even closer. I felt it was important to get the sound right.

"Once we had it down, we started cutting the track. We tried really hard to get the right feel for the song." Apparently, they were successful, because "The Heart of Rock and Roll" peaked at number 6 on the *Billboard* Hot 100 chart.

Another song that would go on the *Sports* album, "I Want a New Drug," wasn't written about drugs, as the title suggested. In fact, it was about finding a new lover. Gaines recalls that at the time, controversy revolved around radio stations playing songs with drug references or connotations. Because this was about the time the so-called War on Drugs was reaching its peak, politicians were urging a ban on any lyrics they construed as being about illegal drugs.

"Once the album was out, the record company began having reservations about releasing the song as a single," Gaines remembers. But the song was released, and like "The Heart of Rock and Roll," it became a top 10 hit, also going to number 6 on the *Billboard* chart. Later, there would be legal difficulties with the song, though not involving politicians.

"Huey had always wanted to do a country song," Gaines says. "As a result, we recorded Hank Williams's 'Honky Tonk Blues.' Also, the song 'If This Is It' was recorded earlier, and it also became a hit single from the album." In fact, "If This Is It" would, like two of the singles before it, go to number 6 on the *Billboard* chart. That made for a total of four singles, with three making the top 10 on *Billboard*. Not surprisingly, the album sold over seven million copies.

"Interestingly enough, Alex Call was recording an album in the studio next door," Gaines remembers. "By coincidence, both Alex and Huey had worked together earlier in a band called Clover. The producer was Ron Nevison, and he had done a lot of work in England around the same time, so Alex and Huey and I would stop by and say hello and hang out. Unfortunately, Nevison acted like a big shot or something. He couldn't even be bothered to say 'hi' or even look at me when we were passing each other in the narrow hallway. After a while I suggested to Huey that we needed to give him a little attitude adjustment.

"As it turned out, Ron had a special chair that had its own container. He actually had it flown in for his sessions. I told Huey we needed to kidnap his chair and hold it for ransom."

Gaines says that after Nevison left one night, he and Lewis went over to the studio where he was working, grabbed the chair, and brought it to their control room. "We got some mic cords and wrapped them around the chair, it as if it were tied up. Then we put on Halloween masks and held a knife to it, like you might hold a knife to a person's throat. We even took some photos and wrote a ransom note. It said, 'If you want your chair back, we will need you to deliver $50,000 and a pound of blow. If you don't, you will never see your chair again.' Then we left the picture and the note on his console."

"When the studio people found out about it, they got real nervous. They were afraid he would get so pissed off he would walk out. When the time came for his session, it was surprisingly quiet. We didn't hear a word from him. Then an hour later, he slams open our door, walks over to us, throws a brown paper bag on our console, and says, 'Here's your ransom. I want my fucking chair back!' Then he leaves."

Nevison had had his assistant make photocopies of several hundred-dollar bills and had filled a baggie with powdered sugar to simulate cocaine.

"He got his chair back," Gaines says. "After that we became friends. We hung out and often did dinner together. So we broke the ice, but I guess it could have gone the other way, too."

After the *Sports* album came out, Paramount Pictures contacted Lewis about doing a song for a film they were shooting called *Ghostbusters*. Lewis and his manager passed on the offer, but when the movie came out, Ray Parker Jr.'s version of the title tune, included in the soundtrack, sounded suspiciously familiar.

"It was a direct steal of 'I Want a New Drug,'" Gaines insists. "Bob [Brown] called a meeting with me and the band, and we played both songs. We were shocked by how close the two were. We decided that we should sue."

Later, the litigants would discover that a letter written to Ray Parker specifically asked him to make his song similar to Huey's. The case would be settled out of court for an undisclosed amount of money.

Another Lewis song that would actually be included in a film soundtrack was "The Power of Love," featured in the movie *Back to the Future.* "I remember that when we were recording it, I thought it was going to be a big hit, and in fact it was. It was never on any of Huey's own albums, but it became a major international hit." In fact, "The Power of Love" would become the first number 1 hit on the *Billboard* Hot 100 chart for Huey Lewis and the News.

"As we were finishing the recording, some of the cast, including the film's main stars Michael J. Fox and Christopher Lloyd, came to the studio for a visit. They brought that special futuristic [DeLorean] car from the movie with them as well."

The song eventually snagged a Grammy nomination, and Lewis even got a part in the movie, playing the high school principal. "He loved it," Gaines recalls, "especially when he's judging a Battle of the Bands audition by Michael J. Fox's character, and he tells the group, 'You're just too darn loud.'

"During the Huey sessions, I would get a Coke and a Snickers bar for my snack on break. As a joke, Huey had my assistant place a Coke and Snickers on all thirty-two channels of the console, with a note saying, 'This should keep you going for a few days.'"

Gaines says that once the *Sports* album was completed, Bob Brown, the band's manager, decided he wasn't happy with Chrysalis, their record label at the time. The company had fired most of its promotion staff and was undergoing a spate of changes.

"You don't want your new record coming out and not being promoted properly," Gaines explains. "We had a meeting about that and it was decided that we wouldn't turn over the record until they had gotten their staff back in place. Bob held the record for a couple of months before releasing it, and I'm glad he did." *Sports* would go on to the number 1 spot on the *Billboard* 200 album chart. It has since been certified seven times platinum.

000

The day after he finished his final session with Huey Lewis, Gaines started working with Pablo Cruise.

"The first time I met the band was when they opened up for Steve Miller," Gaines relates. "They were a rock-pop band based in Marin County. That was also when I first met Bob Brown, Huey Lewis's manager. Pablo Cruise's main driving force was David Jenkins on guitar and vocals, Cory Lerios on keyboards, Steve Price on drums, and Bud Cockrell, who was originally on bass."

The group's first album was released in 1975, but in 1977 they came out with *A Place in the Sun,* which reached number 19 on the charts.

"By 1983, John Pierce and Stef Bernbaum had joined the band after Bud had left. John was a session bass player based in LA and a good fit for the group. John would later join Huey's band.

"The album I recorded with them was called *Out of Our Hands.* I had been in consideration to work with them on the previous album, but [producer] Tom Dowd was chosen instead. I remember that when they were working on it, Tom and I went out for dinner one night. I reminded him about meeting him at Stax, and I said he was one of my heroes. It was nice to even be considered in his league; I thought he was one of the best producers out there."

Gaines mentions that the band wanted to change direction slightly, with Cory Lerios focusing more on synth keyboards. "They still had to stay with what had created their success," Gaines says. "The sessions were fun, and they were all great musicians. Unfortunately, the songs weren't quite as strong, even though they were still very commercial.

"The band was easy to work with because of the various connections between us. I remember once while I was at an interview session with them, the interviewer asked which guy was Pablo. They all pointed at me at the same time. The poor deejay was caught off guard and didn't know whether to ask me a question or not. They died laughing. Ultimately, the recording went well, but it wasn't as successful as some of their past albums.

"A little later, after finishing the project, I got a call from Cory, who had been doing some film scores, even while we were recording the album. He wanted to know if he could borrow my new assistant, Moria Marquis, who I had just brought in from New York. Cory was recording in a small studio around the corner. The project ended up being released as part of the new *Max Headroom* TV show. In fact, Cory ended up getting the whole series. Then he got to do *Baywatch* right after that. I never got Moria back, but I'm happy they both launched an entirely new career. I'm proud of both of them."

Shortly after that, Pablo Cruise disbanded. "Cory and I would later work on a couple of projects together," Gaines says. "One had him helping me with the Neville Brothers, while another involved Melissa Etheridge."

CHAPTER 18

The End of an Era . . .
and the Beginning of a New One

1984

THE RECORD PLANT, which produced so many important albums, was a recurring place of impact in Gaines's career. Even when it changed ownership, he would continue to be involved closely in the music being recorded and distributed from there.

"The Record Plant was sold to a man named Stan Jacox, a businessman from the Apple Valley [Tahoe] area. Before the sale, he approached me to discuss what would happen to me if he bought the studio. He wanted to know what my deal with the previous owner was and whether I would be happy to continue working there. I said I would consider it.

"He didn't have any studio management experience, so he asked if I would accept a small salary and take on the role of general manager. I sort of had that role with Laurie, the previous owner, because I was involved in some of the management decisions." Gaines remembers having some reservations about the new ownership, especially when he learned that Jacox had put down cash for the deposit and had paid cash for the purchase. "Nobody walks around with that kind of cash," Gaines says. "I wouldn't sign a contract for that reason."

Gaines recalls that Jacox didn't come to the studio every day, but he did come in fairly often. In the meantime, some changes did take place. "We ended up taking what we called the Pit—the 'C' studio—and making it a normal studio by installing a new console. Stan made some cosmetic changes inside the building as well. He was schooled in electronics, so he liked messing around with the gear. After a couple of months, he decided to take me, our chief engineer, and himself to the AES [Audio Engineering Society] trade show in New York to check out some new consoles and other studio gear."

The Record Plant group stayed at the famous Helmsley Park Lane Hotel. Cardinal Cook, the Roman Catholic archbishop of New York from 1968 to 1984, had just passed away, and the cathedral was just across the street from the hotel. "The entire hotel was filled with dignitaries and their security," Gaines remembers. "Stan decided he wanted to buy a short-waisted mink coat. As he was purchasing his coat, he got into a conversation with the sales lady and ended up talking her into coming to work for us. We ended up hiring a studio manager who had never been in a studio." Despite Gaines's concerns at the time, he recalls that the new hire ended up being a valuable assistant.

"I remember that the hotel bar wouldn't let us in because we were wearing jeans and Stan had his mink coat. At that point, Ms. Helmsley herself came by and loaned us some sport coats to wear. As we were checking out, we were handed a bill for fifteen hundred dollars. Stan reached into his briefcase and started counting out hundred-dollar bills. I put my hand on his and suggested that he let me put the charge on my credit card because it would look better that way."

One of the first sessions in the redesigned studio C was for John Fogerty, previously the lead singer and guitarist and principal songwriter for Creedence Clearwater Revival. "He had approached me a few weeks earlier about working with him," Gaines explains. "For years, he had been waiting out his contract with Fantasy Records. He and the label had had a big falling out over some money issues. I never learned all the details, but suffice it to say that Creedence Clearwater Revival had lost a considerable amount of money, and John blamed it on bad advice from Fantasy. As a result, John decided to just wait them out before he would start recording again."

"John had a small studio space at his house and had already begun some preproduction on the project. He played all the instruments. Unfortunately, I was in the middle of a project with a group called Con Funk Shun, and I wasn't available to do it. I suggested he use my assistant, Jeffery Norman. They set up the room so John could play any instrument at any time. I had given him a rate to get the studio going, and they settled in."

Fogerty ended up recording for a couple of weeks, and then the album was mixed. Upon release, it was titled *Centerfield*, and it became Fogerty's first official solo album following the demise of Creedence Clearwater Revival.

"One of the songs was called "Zanz Kant Danz," Gaines remembers. "The song is about Saul Zaentz, one of the owners of the Fantasy label. In the lyric, John says, 'Zanz can't dance, but he will steal your money.' The record was initially pressed with that title and the offending lyric. Saul threatened to sue him over it, so John came back into the studio and came up with a new lyric while changing the title to 'Vanz Kant Danz.' He also changed the line to 'Vanz' instead of 'Zanz,' and then rereleased that album. It didn't matter. Saul sued him again, this time for plagiarism. He said the song sounded too close to a Creedence song."

No surprise there, according to Gaines. "After all, John *was* the voice of CCR. Remember, too, the reason I moved to San Francisco was to replace Russ Gary, the man who had recorded Creedence. So here I was, hanging out with John in our kitchen and hearing all his stories. I told him one time, 'You don't know how many quarters I put in jukeboxes because of you.'"

Despite the legal scuffle over "Vanz Kant Danz" and its previous iteration, *Centerfield* proved to be a very successful comeback album, selling over a million copies. "John gave me a beautiful leather jacket with 'Centerfield' embossed on it as a thank-you gift," Gaines says proudly. "I still have that jacket."

000

Meanwhile, Gaines was working with Con Funk Shun. The group had been signed by Estelle Axton, a part owner of Stax Studios, to her own Fretone label in 1973. A funk band from the Bay Area that had moved to Memphis for a short time to become part of the Stax Studios rhythm sections, the group had recorded some successful records and even had a few hits. The band's producer was Maurice Starr [a stage name for Larry Curtis Johnson], who formed and recorded New Edition, New Kids on the Block, and several other "boy bands."

The Con Funk Shun album Gaines worked on was called *Electric Lady*, and he, along with a few other producers, would subsequently be involved with the record, since it was normal in those days, according to Gaines, to have several people doing production.

"The band was very talented," Gaines says. "I loved working with them, especially Michael Cooper [rhythm guitarist and singer] and Felton Pilate II [lead singer]. Felton and I went on to work on several projects later on. Maurice, the producer, had an incredible memory. He could play you a little bit of practically any song. We had a keyboard set up in the control room, and we tested him. Damned if we could find even one song he didn't know.

"When he arrived at the session one day, he had a lady friend with him.

They were staying at the band house. Around the third night he was there, he called me at home, saying he and the girlfriend had gotten into an argument, and she had threatened him with a knife. One of them called the police and when they got there, they told him he might have to go to jail. I couldn't believe what I was hearing."

Gaines says he got on the phone with the police and explained to them who Starr was and why he was there. "I pleaded with them to not take him in. Fortunately, they gave them both a stern warning that they had better calm down, or else."

Starr was also working with Gaines on demos and projects for other artists during those recordings. "Some mornings we would do demos for New Edition or [jazz trumpeter] Tom Browne and then spend time recording Con Funk Shun the rest of the day. Tom was from the East Coast, and he would occasionally come out west to work a few days. Maurice had a brother in Boston who had his own studio, so some things could be done there and some things done at the Plant."

Starr's nickname was "The General." Gaines recalls that he even dressed like the kind of general you might see in what used to be called a third-world country. "When we were mixing, he showed me some things I had never seen before, so I learned some new tricks."

000

While at the Record Plant, Gaines was briefly involved in another Santana project, an album called *Beyond Appearances*. The album was being produced by Val Garay, who generally worked from Studio One, a location he owned in Los Angeles. Garay accumulated a number of credits, including work with Kim Carnes ("Bette Davis Eyes"), James Taylor, and Linda Ronstadt, among many others.

The Santana album had been started at Studio One, then moved to the Record Plant to finish the overdubs. Garay brought his engineers with him. "Val was another guy who wasn't a superfriendly person to me," Gaines maintains. "Because I had worked with Carlos [Santana] previously, I guess he saw me as some sort of threat. When we passed each other in the hallway, he would purposely avoid me.

"Some members of the crew and various musicians in the band expressed some problems with his way of doing things. Two crew guys and the conga player were even barred from the control room. As a joke, the crew got a map of Hollywood, and in the middle of it they stuck a photo of Garay with a star and a caption that said 'Mr. Hollywood.' They also had a number system that tallied the days he was on time and the days he was late. They put it on the wall at the entrance of the studio, and naturally, he wasn't too happy about it. He complained about the being late part, but I think he sort of liked the 'Mr. Hollywood' reference.

"Later, when it came time to mix, he would send mixes to Carlos so he could listen to them. Carlos apparently didn't like some of them, so he called me and asked if I would make some good rough mixes on two of the songs to show Val how Santana should sound. However, Val had a clause in his contract that specified he had two chances to mix before there were any changes.

"I mixed a couple of songs by accentuating the percussion and making it more stereo friendly. My mix was just to show Garay what it should sound like; it definitely wasn't supposed to be the final version. Still, I knew what Carlos would probably want. So Carlos sent them to Val and told him that one of the songs would make it to the album. I'm sure Val was infuriated over this, but regardless, I got a mix on the record."

Later, Gaines would have one more interaction with Garay, when working with Bruce Hornsby. In the meantime, another Santana project was waiting in the wings.

000

The album was a solo project that didn't involve the band. It was dubbed *Blues for Salvador*, and it was named for Santana's son, Salvador. It was also the third project done in the Record Plant's new C studio.

"I was executive producer and engineer on most of this project," Gaines explains. "Tony Williams [drummer for Miles Davis, Freddie Hubbard, Herbie Hancock, and others] and Alphonso Johnson [bassist for Weather Report, Phil Collins, and others] were part of the rhythm section, along with singers Greg Walker, Alex Ligertwood, and Graham Lear, as well as conga player Armando Peraza and [drummer] Buddy Miles. Working with some of these guys was great for me. They were some of the most elite players around."

Tony Williams was a prodigious drummer, Gaines remembers, especially for jazz and fusion music. However, he wasn't the easiest guy to get drum sounds with, according to Gaines. "When I asked him to go all around the drums for level and tone, he did so one time, then put his drumsticks down and picked up the newspaper," Gaines says. "Most of the time, we would need to spend at least fifteen to twenty minutes minimum to get our EQ [equalization] and [volume] levels, especially since we were using a rented drum set. So, Williams and Carlos's front-of-house mixer kind of got into a little skirmish over levels. That certainly didn't go over well while we were trying to get things started. Also, as he played, he would often stand up. I had never seen anything like that before with a drummer. Certainly, the kick [bass] drum is rarely played like that. I guess it was a jazz thing I didn't know about."

A few of the tracks for the album originated from previous recordings, Gaines says. The instrumental track "Blues for Salvador" would go on to win a Grammy for Best Instrumental Track, providing Carlos Santana with his first Grammy. Later, Gaines was partially involved in a Santana band project called *Freedom*. His role was to oversee overdubs and do some mixing.

"There were nine former Santana band members guesting on the album," Gaines recalls, "including some of my favorites: blues great Junior Wells, drummers Buddy Miles and Chester Thompson, bassist Alphonso Johnson, and keyboard players Gregg Rolie and Tom Coster."

Freedom found Santana going back to his seminal Latin rock sound and away from the more pop-oriented approach of *Beyond Appearances*. The album would make it only to number 95 on the charts. Nevertheless, Gaines would take the next stage of his career journey with a band by the same name.

CHAPTER 19

A New Journey—with Journey

1984–1985

JOURNEY—WITH STEVE PERRY on lead vocals, Neal Schon on lead guitar, Jonathan Cain on keyboards, Steve Smith on drums, and Ross Valory on bass—had already achieved substantial success with chart-topping hits like "Don't Stop Believing" and "Open Arms," as well as albums that reached the first (*Escape*) and second (*Frontiers*) positions on the *Billboard* 200 list. For their newest album, Gaines was asked to be the engineer and associate producer, while Steve Perry took on the role of producer.

Perry was coming off a solo album called *Street Talk*, which he had produced and paid for himself. He had some songs that he wanted to record without the band. CBS agreed to release it and it became a big hit, selling over two million copies.

"A lot of the songs were inspired by his relationship with a woman named Sherrie Stafford," Gaines explains. "That's where the big hit single 'Oh Sherrie' came from. After the relationship ended, Steve took it pretty hard. By the time I met him, he was almost a recluse. As we were working on the album, I made a point of taking him out with me and we began hanging out a lot together. Also, at this point I think Steve wanted a little more control of the band."

At this time, the group was coming off a two-year hiatus following the release of their album *Frontiers* and the subsequent touring that supported it. "When we started with the tracking, Ross Valory, the bassist, was struggling a little bit," Gaines reflects. "I don't think he had played all that much during their long time off. Steve Perry, though known mainly as a vocalist, is really a singing drummer," Gaines continues. "So he was really into getting the precise feel on the tracks. He was a big fan of Sam Cook and other big soul singers, even though he was in a rock band. A week into the tracking, he came to me and told me that he wanted to replace Ross. He didn't think the bass feel was right for the tracks."

Perry brought in Bob Glaub, an LA session player who had worked in John Fogerty's band, to replace Valory. At this point, Gaines explains, the agreement was that Ross Valory would still be in the band but would not play on the album.

"We tracked around fourteen songs. After about another week, Steve Perry approached me again and said, 'Jim, I don't think I can sing correctly on these tracks.' When I asked why, he said that the drums felt a little too much on the front side of the beat.

"The thing was, the band's drummer, Steve Smith, was more of a jazz drummer than a straight rock player. Normally, jazz guys play more on top of the groove, whereas soul or R&B drummers play on the back side. Steve Perry came from the latter camp. On the other hand, Steve Smith had recorded several jazz albums during the band's time off."

When Gaines asked Perry what he wanted to do, he said, "We need to start over." This was after Gaines and the group had already spent nearly three weeks working on the album.

"The night Perry told Smith that he wanted to start over but still have Smith in the band, things got very emotional. As we were listening to this conversation, half of us were crying. Steve Smith is a great guy, and I hated to see him go."

"We ended up bringing in Randy Jackson on bass along with Glaub, and on drums, we got Larrie Londin from Nashville. And then we started over. Randy was originally a San Francisco player who had been working quite a bit for Narada Michael Walden, as well as doing sessions for Aretha Franklin and Mariah Carey. He had been an early part of the Motown studio stable, as well as a top Nashville player."

Fortunately, Gaines says, the new rhythm section worked out really well, and the tracking progressed very nicely. Steve Perry was happy.

"Jonathan Cain had a piano that was set up to send MIDI information to a synthesizer as he played. That was something new to me, but I loved it.

Guitarist Neal Schon was also playing great, as usual. He was one of those players who can get sounds that are almost like vocal phrasing. Plus, he and I had a history; I had worked with him since he was sixteen years old."

Gaines remembers that Larrie Londin was "like a drum machine" for timing, but he could also set up the groove very soulfully. "He was also a lot of fun, but he was dealing with some health issues. As a result of those problems, he wouldn't be able to tour with the band later on."

Gaines brought his own technique and technology to the sessions. "I was using my Yamaha NS-10 speakers, which the band loved," he recalls. "They wanted some pairs for themselves, so I placed an order for ten new pairs. This was actually the second order of this size I had placed, because I had bought Huey Lewis's guys the same amount. The distributor called me and asked me if I wanted to be a rep distributor for him, because I was buying more than the local guys. I said that I was just trying to keep some clients happy."

Gaines has observed that most bands are run very democratically. Everyone has a say and the opportunity to voice an opinion. However, he also points out that while that's a good intention, it doesn't always work so well in the studio. "In Journey's case, it was good, except that everyone wanted to do their part right away," he reflects. "It was kind of like children who want things now. So, to help determine the order for who would be next, I bought one of those take-a-ticket machines like you'd see at a deli counter or a store where you have to wait to be served. It was like, 'Number four, you're up next.' I set it up next to the console and everyone got into the idea of getting a number. It was fun, and it worked so well that I used it for some of my future projects as well."

As Journey returned to working on tracks for the new album, Gaines got a call from an equipment manufacturer, Monster Cable. The company wanted Gaines to ask the band whether it could bring in some microphones and instrument cable for Journey to use in exchange for an endorsement deal.

"Of course, everyone wants gear that's supposedly free. So, Monster brought a couple of boxes of cables in, and we tried using them. Their business was just getting started at this point. I didn't care for some of them because they were too microphonic, picking up on the unwanted low end.

"Towards the end of the overdub sessions, they called me and asked how we liked them. I freely shared my thoughts, after which they said they would be coming over to get their cables back. However, the band and I thought that if you use endorsement equipment, you get to keep it. In fact, the band had divided up the cables and taken them home."

Gaines had to get the band's manager involved in order get the matter straightened out. "Later, when our mixer, Bob Clearmountain, was getting ready to do the mix, he gave me a call and asked, 'Who in the hell are these Monster Cable people?' He sounded very agitated. I thought to myself, 'Oh no!'

"Bob told me that they had called Bearsville Studios, who had just revamped their studios according to Bob's specifications. Apparently, the company had told them that they had to rewire their studio with Monster cables, because Journey was endorsing their product. Naturally, Bob was furious."

Gaines explained the background to Clearmountain, including his experience with the equipment. "We both agreed, to hell with those people. I never bought a Monster cable after that."

Meanwhile, Gaines was trying to help Steve Perry get over his breakup trauma. "I was trying to get Steve out of the house so we could relax and have dinner together," he relates. "I could see he needed a friend outside of the band. He was also on a strict diet during the recording, so he didn't feel comfortable going out to eat. However, I insisted."

On one of their nights out, Gaines and Perry went to see Gallagher, the comedian. When Gallagher's management found out that they were coming, they gave Gaines and Perry front-row seats.

"Now, you really didn't want to be in the front row at a Gallagher concert, because his routine involved this thing where he took this big hammer that he called a 'Sledge-O-Matic' and used it to smash a watermelon, sending parts of the watermelon throughout the first few rows." Fortunately, the comedian's management had given Gaines and Perry a plastic sheet for cover during this part of the show. It was still a mess, Gaines says, but they enjoyed the show.

"After the show, Steve and I along with Gallagher and some of his people went out to one of my favorite watering holes. Of course, when people recognized Steve and Gallagher, they came over to ask for autographs. Steve would smile and sign them, but Gallagher refused to sign an autograph for anyone. I've been with and around a lot of famous people, and that's one thing that bugs me. I think you should greet fans in a friendly way and try to be nice. It would be different if the fans were being disrespectful, but if they are being nice, it's not right to give them the brush-off."

During the recording sessions, Perry's mother was very ill as a result of a stroke that had left her mostly paralyzed and unable to speak. Gaines says that Steve went to see her at her home in Fresno, California, as often as he could.

"One day he told me that he wanted to fly her up on a private flight to Reno," Gaines remembers. "Steve wanted to take her to Caesar's Palace, and he wanted to know if I would like to go as well. The Everly Brothers were playing there, and his mom loved them, he said.

"So we flew down and picked her up, along with her nurse and his stepdad, and we flew to Reno. His mother's face lit up as we were checking in. We took her to the slot machines, and I put some money in. Then we put her hand on the lever so she could pull it down. What a joy it was, watching her smile and laugh.

"Jonathan Cain, the keyboard player, and his brother had driven to Reno as well, so we all had dinner and enjoyed some great seats for the show. Steve had gone backstage to meet with the Everlys and requested that they sing 'Cathy's Clown,' one of his mom's favorites, and dedicate it to her. When it came time for the song, they made the announcement and the dedication and started singing. She was so happy, she started crying and moaning with delight. That caused the rest of us to start crying as well. It was quite an emotional moment."

After the show, Gaines, Perry, and the rest of the entourage went backstage and met the brothers and also saw their friend and drummer Larrie Londin, who was also playing drums for the Everly Brothers show. Later, after getting Perry's mother settled in her room, Gaines and the others went down to the casino floor to gamble and enjoy each other's company.

"Jonathan's brother, who was also a drummer, had some drumsticks poking out of his back pocket. Unfortunately, he backed into a lady who had a drink in her hand, jabbing her in the butt. As a result, she sent her drink flying, and it ended up on the blackjack table where we were situated. Naturally, the pit boss was not impressed. They had to shut down the table and get it dried off. We were asked to leave the area."

Gaines says he is still grateful that he was able to take this trip with Steve Perry, because his mother passed away not too long afterward. "Steve and I became very close during that time."

CHAPTER 20

Here Come the Feds

1985

GAINES AND COMPANY were working on the final overdubs for the Journey project at the studio, only to receive a very unexpected and unwelcome interruption, courtesy of the federal government.

"I was driving into the parking lot early one morning and I noticed a lot of cars were there, especially for that time of day," Gaines remembers. "As I was walking to the front door, out of nowhere I found myself surrounded by police, the DEA, sheriff's deputies, and law enforcement officials of all varieties. They stopped me and asked me who I was. I explained that I worked at the studio, and once I did, they immediately grabbed me by my arms and told me that we needed to go inside and talk. They led me to my office, where I found a DEA agent waiting for me."

Gaines was told that the owner, Stan Jacox, had been arrested and charged with manufacturing amphetamines, and as a result the law enforcement officials had confiscated the building and everything in it. They suspected that some of the manufacturing had been taking place at the studio.

"It was kind of like what you see in the movies, with police and agents everywhere," Gaines muses. "My studio manager and chief engineer were being questioned in another office. We weren't allowed to speak to one another. The head agent was one of the coldest people I ever met. His eyes would stare right through you. Once he started questioning me, he began sharing facts and conversations that he could only know if either my phone or Stan's had been tapped. In fact, I remember thinking a couple of times, before all this happened, that something was wrong with my phone. So in retrospect, it could actually have been mine."

Gaines says that the agents went through everything in the building, including all the equipment containers of the three different artists who were working in the studio at that time. "Eventually, after an hour or two of questioning," Gaines says, "I told the head guy that I had sessions scheduled that day and that I needed to get on the phone, call the artists, and cancel them. We also needed to get the bands' gear and master tapes out of the building. In fact, it was very strange, having the artists and crews show up to move their gear. They all wanted to know what was going on and what was going to happen to the studio."

Gaines noticed that the authorities had gone through all the bands' road cases in search of drugs, but fortunately, nothing was found. "Even as I was assembling tapes, they felt compelled to open every box to make sure nothing was hidden in them. Needless to say, these guys weren't very friendly towards me or my staff. But by the end of the day we had managed to get everyone's gear out. Eventually, after getting all of our personal stuff and all my own gear out, the studio was shut down. They assigned two security people to live in the studio for nearly a year."

After the studio had been shuttered for nearly twelve months, Gaines got a call from the head law enforcement official, asking him whether he would consider opening up the studio after signing an exclusive contract. In effect, the federal government would be his employer.

"I told him very clearly, 'Listen, if my clients found out that I was employed by the Feds, I would never work again.' I suggested that they hire my staff back and make my former secretary the studio manager. If all that was done, I would consider bringing back in some business. By this time, the studio had come to be known as Club Fed," Gaines says with a smile.

The authorities agreed to Gaines's proposal, and the studio was reopened. Gaines became its first client when he brought in Santana.

"It was a mess in there," Gaines recalls. "The security guards had trashed the place while they were staying there. It took time to get the gear back in shape as well."

Gaines remembers that during one of the first sessions back in the studio, it was raining outside. "As I was mixing, water was leaking over the console. I had to find some big sheets of plastic and make a barrier between the water from the roof and my now increasingly damp console. Of course, the government doesn't like spending any money on a place that has been confiscated, but I told them they had to fix that roof or I was leaving."

It took some time to get other artists to return to the studio because it was legally still owned by the authorities. "When I got Santana to come and record, MTV came and set up in the control room to tape the event. They captured the back of my head while filming the session—thank goodness I still had hair." With his typical self-deprecating humor, Gaines counts the taping by MTV as his "fifteen minutes of fame." As usual, though, this undersells his actual reputation, as future events would prove.

Jim Gaines and Sandy Carroll Gaines getting brass notes on Beale Street. *Photograph by Bob Taylor.*

Celia and Bernard Purdie with Gaines at Gaines's studio. *Photograph by Barbara Blue.*

Gaines and Rob Sudduth, sax player from Huey's band. *Photograph by Jody Stevens.*

Gaines, Huey Lewis, and John Fry from Ardent getting brass notes. *Photograph by Bob Taylor.*

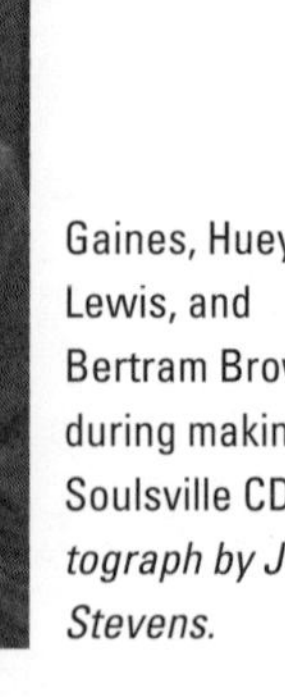

Gaines, Huey Lewis, and Bertram Brown during making of Soulsville CD. *Photograph by Jody Stevens.*

5.Bill Ellis, Gaines, and Sandy at Saint Michael's College in Vermont, giving a seminar on the blues. Photograph by Julie Ellis.

7.Gaines with Huey Lewis's band and engineers at Ardent. Photograph by Jody Stevens.

8.Tone (engineer), Carlos Santana, unknown producer, and Gaines at Fantasy Studios.

9.Gaines in his domain: the control booth of Studio B at the Plant, mid-1980s.

10.Gaines at the Plant, mid-1980s.

11.Rocky Athas and Gaines. *Photograph by Sandy Carroll Gaines.*

12.A young Gaines at Ardent. *Photograph by Jody Stevens.*

13.A young Carlos San-
tana and Gaines at the
Automatt, around 1980.

14.Sandy and Gaines
in the remote truck
recording Walter Trout
at the famous Parad-
iso club in Amsterdam.
*Photograph by Ira
Leslie.*

15.Gaines and Al Kapone, lead singer from Mafia 666, in Memphis. P*hotograph by Sandy Carroll Gaines.*

16.Gaines, David Porter, and Al Bell at the new Stax. *Photograph by Bob Taylor.*

17. Gaines and David Porter at the new Stax. Photograph by Bob Taylor.

18. Gaines and Steve Miller at a Grammy event, where they talked about making *Fly Like an Eagle*.

19George Thorogood and Gaines. *Photograph by Maria Thorogood.*

20.Jeff Simon (drummer for George Thorogood), Elvin Bishop, and Gaines. *Photograph by Sandy Carroll Gaines.*

22.A thoughtful Gaines observes a session at the Plant, mid-1980s.

21.Another brass note. *Photograph by Ken Hall.*

23.Session with Royal Southern Brotherhood, Devon Allman playing guitar. Recording at Dockside Studio. Lafayette La.

24.Gaines gets an impromptu "guitar lesson" from Stevie Ray Vaughan, 1989.

25.Gaines in 2018. *Photograph courtesy of Cry Rock.*

26.Gaines and Albert Collins while making Iceman CD, ca. 1994.

27.Jim Gaines. *Photograph by Sabrina Bordenkircher.*

<Extra1>Gaines at work in his studio. *Photograph by Sandy Carroll Gaines.*

CHAPTER 21

More Hits from Huey

1986

WHILE GAINES WOULD RECORD in a variety of studios over the course of his career, the Plant somehow always managed to lure him back. "The Plant had settled back to more of a normal recording environment," Gaines recalls. "After an artist scores a big hit, they typically analyze each song. The thought is that another song that sounds similar to the hit is needed to keep the streak going. As a result, each song that's being looked at is compared in hopes of duplicating that success again.

"In reality, though, it really doesn't work that way. If anything, you need to create some new songs that sound fresh, but still maintain your sound and style. Unfortunately, most bands and managers find it hard to think like that."

Finding himself back at the Plant with Huey Lewis in the studio felt like coming home, Gaines says. "I felt comfortable there. The recording was going well, but things were going slower than normal. While we were recording, the band often had to run out to do a few shows. In that case, it always takes a while to get things restarted and back up to speed after they take that break." The band was also trying to find that next big hit.

Gaines remembers that they started changing their food orders, and as a result the quality of the cuisine went up a couple of notches. "Before, we would just order some fast food. But after we had such big hits ["I Want a

New Drug," "Do You Believe," "Power of Love," and others], we decided we could afford to order some nice, expensive meals. We were getting these great dinners brought in, but not keeping track of the cost. One day, Bob Brown, Huey's manager, came in and informed us that the new eating habits had to change. He told us we had already spent ten thousand dollars on food. We couldn't believe it." From that point forward, Gaines, his crew, and the band were cut off from the expensive restaurants.

The band's keyboard player, Sean Hopper, was trying out some new equipment. "At that time, new keyboards were coming out almost daily," Gaines recalls. "Sean loved his new toys, but in my opinion, he really is a great Hammond B3 [organ] player. That's what he does best."

Gaines also says that guitarist Chris Hayes was always solid in his playing as well, and that his songwriting was top-notch. "I loved working with him. Mario [Cipollina], the bass player, was always a great guy and a lot of fun. However, after the album came out, he would end up leaving the band. I also recall that guitarist and saxophone player Johnny Colla was always the stable force in the group, especially when it came to the arrangements and vocal parts. He got the best out of Huey's vocals. Sometimes Huey would want to oversing his vocals, but Johnny and I would pull him back." Gaines also remembers that Colla had an apartment over a local pool hall, and that "he was an excellent pool player. I wish I could have been half as good as he was."

After the success of the *Sports* album, everyone in the band had bought new cars, new equipment, and even new houses. "It was fun watching the success the band attained, because when I first met them," Gaines says, "half of them lived together in one house." Gaines also remembers that formerly, when he and Huey Lewis went out to eat, none of the other diners paid any attention. "Now, however, when we took our dates out, we would have to find a place where he wouldn't get mobbed by fans."

When Gaines began work on Huey Lewis's 1986 *Fore!* album, some songs were still being considered, and some new material and other originals were being completed. "Jacob's Ladder," written by Bruce Hornsby, had been previously considered for the *Sports* album but was selected for *Fore!* and would reach the top slot on the *Billboard* Hot 100 in 1987, the band's third number 1 hit.

"'Hip to Be Square' had some interesting backup vocals," Gaines says. "Several members of the San Francisco 49ers football team sang background parts, including Joe Montana, Dwight Clark, and Ronnie Lott. The song was written by Bill Gibson, Sean Hopper, and Huey himself. It would go on to become a big radio hit.

"We had recorded 'Stuck with You' between albums," Gaines says. "The song was written by Huey and Chris Hayes. It also became a number one record; radio stations and listeners loved that song." "Simple as That" was written by Steve Kupka and Emilio Castillo from Tower of Power. "That was a great collaboration," Gaines notes. Ultimately, *Fore!* was a huge hit, selling several million records, certifying three times platinum, and reaching the top spot on the *Billboard* album charts.

The ABCs of KBC

1986

JUST AS GAINES WAS FINISHING the Huey Lewis project, the KBC band asked him to work on their new album. KBC was a spin-off of Jefferson Airplane, whose members included Paul Kantner, Marty Balin, and Jack Casady, all original members of the Airplane lineup.

"I had to give KBC a start date, so I went to Huey and the band and asked when we might be done with our work on *Fore!*," Gaines explains. "Huey and Bob gave me a date when they were sure that they would be done, while taking their touring schedule into account. I would give myself two weeks between albums either for time off or just to make sure the previous project was actually done."

The schedule was set. The plan called for Huey to go to New York and have Bob Clearmountain do the mix. Of course, plans often change.

"I had told Clive Davis of Arista Records, the label for KBC, when my start time would be, and that locked me in," Gaines says. "Unfortunately, the week before we were due to start the new project, Huey told me that he needed more time. There were more overdubs to be done, and he also informed me that Bob Clearmountain wanted too much money to do the mix. I was stuck.

"I told him that I couldn't change my schedule, but that I would let my assistant Bob Missbach finish up the overdubs that were left to do. Huey said that they would get Bob's assistant in New York to take over the mix. At that point we were all good." Lewis took care of getting the mix done and Gaines began tracking KBC.

But it would prove to be not so simple as that. "Three or four days in, I got a panicked phone call from Huey after only one day of mixing. He was stressed out. He told me they spent the entire first day working on the kick drum sound. Clearmountain would normally get one to two songs finished per day, but apparently his assistant was a long way from accomplishing that.

"Huey told me that I would have to drop everything and fly to New York to take over the mixing. I told him, 'Huey, I just started tracking here, and Clive Davis will probably fire me if I stop now.' But Huey insisted. I suggested instead that I fly Bob Missbach to New York and let him mix, and if that didn't work, we would have to find another solution."

Gaines sent Missbach to finish the mix for Huey. Bob had never mixed an entire album, but he had been at Gaines's side while the album was being recorded, so he knew the band and the material. To everyone's relief, he was able to finish the album.

Even so, the situation created a rift between Lewis and Gaines that lasted almost twenty years. "He felt like I had let him down," Gaines says. "If there had been any other project and any other record company involved, I would have stopped and helped him. To tell the truth, I regret to this day that I made that choice. We had been so close, both personally and professionally, and it hurt me for a long time."

Twenty years later Gaines and Lewis would do one more project together: Lewis's *Soulsville* album, which would be released in Memphis. "Huey was also there for me when blues singer Sandy Carroll and I got our Beale Street Brass Notes on the Walk of Fame," Gaines remembers. "We went to a bar afterwards, cleared the air, and rekindled our friendship—thank God."

000

KBC, whose name was drawn from the first letters of the last names of the band's founders, Paul Kantner, Marty Balin, and Jack Casady, also featured the talents of guitarist Slick Aguilar, Keith Crossan on sax, Tim Gorman on keyboards, and Darrell Verdusco on drums. "Before I started the project with them," Gaines says, "I had gone to New York to meet with Clive Davis and get his blessing. With the input of their manager Vincent Lynch, we were able to schedule a start time."

Gaines describes Clive Davis as "a singles kind of guy. He was always looking for songs that would do well on the radio and morph into hits." However, as Gaines notes, the band was pursuing a more album-oriented project. Hits were definitely in the group's lineage, however. Jefferson Airplane contributed "Somebody to Love" (which peaked in fifth place on the *Billboard* chart in June 1967) and "White Rabbit" (number 8 on the charts in July of the same year), both songs featuring the inimitable vocal stylings of Grace Slick. Jefferson Starship, which spun off from Airplane, put out "Miracles," which reached the number 3 spot in October 1975. However, at this point eleven years later, Kantner had recently left Starship, following the departure of Balin and Casady. Kantner wanted to go back more toward the original sound that Jefferson Airplane had created early on, before its Starship incarnation pushed the group in a more pop-oriented direction.

Kantner had helped found the original Airplane with Balin, Slick, Casady, blues guitarist Jorma Kaukonen, and drummer Spencer Dryden (who also played for New Riders of the Purple Sage). The group was named after Kantner's dog, Jefferson. Once he left the band, a legal battle erupted over the name, which Kantner claimed he had coined. He sued and, according to his telling, he won. He once said that he had never really registered the name, but the other members of the group thought he had. At any rate, he got a settlement.

"Paul Kantner was one of those writers that sometimes likes to tell a long story in his songs," Gaines said. "One of the songs he wrote for the KBC album was called 'America.' It was originally fifteen minutes long. Of course, vinyl records could only hold fifteen to sixteen minutes of recorded time per side, so that one song would have taken up the entire side. I told Paul that we would have to cut the song down in order to get additional songs on that side of the album. He didn't want to do that, but he said we had no choice; we would just have to do a double album." Arista, the record company, refused. "They said that wasn't an option for a debut record," Gaines says. The version of "America" that was pressed on the album came in at six minutes and eighteen seconds.

"Now, Paul was a very interesting guy," Gaines remembers. "He was well read, very bright, and personally invested in a lot of political philosophy. He was friends with all the political heavyweights at that time, including Dianne Feinstein, who was mayor of San Francisco. They loved hanging with him.

"He was also a big pot smoker who toked some of the biggest joints I've ever seen. And he always had the best pot around. I remember going to the 'Airplane House,' their office in San Francisco's Haight district. It was quite an intriguing place, and it held lots of great memorabilia. Naturally, there were lots of interesting people always hanging around. I remember getting calls from the head marshal, who would come over fairly often and ask me to please have Paul stay in the studio when he smoked his joints. He said that they had other marshals going over there at times, and it didn't look good to see Paul roaming around the building, openly smoking his weed. I told the marshal, 'Heck, he hangs out with the mayor, city councilmen, and senators, and he smokes dope with them. So he's not going to stop here.'"

Gaines remembers that Kantner had a different style of guitar playing from most people he had worked with. "He kinda attacked or banged on it while he played. Of course, that made it difficult to keep in tune."

Gaines also recalls, "Jack Casady was a great bass player and a fun person to hang out with. He had somewhat matured from the time I first met him in the Heider [record studio] days. He was one of the steady anchors for the band, and he helped make the session a great time."

Gaines remembers Tim Gorman as an excellent keyboard player and one of the nicest guys he ever met. "He also had one of the new Moog keyboards that had come out at that time, and it was very versatile. Tim had toured with The Who for a while, and we would later work together on several other projects.

"Slick Aguilar—whose real name was Mark—was a very good guitar player, and he made a good addition to the band. Likewise, Darrell was a perfect drummer for the group. His style fit the music very well, and his rock feel was just right.

"I had worked with Keith [Crossan] before, and I would work with him later in the Tommy Castro band. He's always a lot of fun and very positive. I loved his playing.

"Marty Balin was a terrific great singer, but I always felt that he was a little insecure in his vocals sometimes when he was in the studio. However, he did have his own style that worked well for him. When he was recording his vocals, he would want to strap on his guitar and hand-hold the microphone. Now, that's okay for live performance, but holding a ten-thousand-dollar microphone with a guitar dangling from his neck was not something the studio wanted. He was also into some mystical kinds of things. He told me he had a pyramid built into his attic—or maybe he called it his 'upper room'—at home, and that was where he meditated."

Gaines remembers that Balin was always sharply dressed, whether in a tennis outfit or just regular street clothes. "He would play tennis most mornings down the street from the studio, so it was no surprise when he would show up in his 'GQ' tennis outfits. But when it came time for him to sing, he always found an excuse not to. I remember he came in on the last day that we were tracking vocals and informed me that he couldn't sing. I asked why, and he said that he had played tennis so badly that morning that he yelled at himself and blew out his voice. Later, in New York, when we were mixing the album, I was talking to John Boylan and telling him that story. He told me that Balin had said the same thing to him. We both cracked up."

They eventually got Balin's vocals for the album, Gaines reports.

"John Boylan was brought in to do a couple of songs that Clive had wanted to get done. John was a great producer with lots of hits under his belt, so the label wanted to try and get a single with him. I think he ended up with one song on the album."

Gaines recalls that though the tracking went smoothly, one really interesting thing happened. "When Clive Davis, who was president of the Arista label, found a demo of a song he liked, he played it over and over and fell in love with it, just the way it was. We call this 'the danger of the demo.' It happens to all of us at some point or another. So we had a song for KBC that fell into that category. The original demo had some rough, out-of-time drum parts and some rough, out-of-tune vocals. After all, usually when a band is roughing songs out for a demo, there are a lot of loose parts.

"So when we recut the song for the album, naturally we had made it more musically correct. When I sent it to Clive, he didn't like it. He said he wanted it like the original demo. So I ended up taking the demo, fixing the drums a little bit, and kind of cleaning up the vocals. Then I sent it back. Again he said, 'No, I want it to sound like the demo.'

"I said, 'It is the demo!' I don't think Clive liked me after that. It's not a good idea to challenge the record company president, but I had to prove a point."

Gaines says that when he went to New York to mix the record with Frank Filipetti, there was a big setup for the mixing waiting for them. Frank, he says, used a lot of outboard gear. Filipetti was a seasoned mixer, having worked on Foreigner's number 1 tune "I Wanna Know What Love Is" and other hits. He would go on to win five Grammy Awards for work on various soundtrack recordings, including *The Color Purple*, *The Book of Mormon*, and *Spamalot*.

"Bruce Springsteen and Bob Clearmountain were working at night after us in the same studio. We went past our studio time on a few occasions, and

I would have to ask them to please give me one more hour to finish up. They were nice about it and said they understood, and so they gave us the little extra time we needed." This was also when Gaines met Moria Marquis, whom he would eventually hire as his assistant and bring to the Record Plant.

The KBC band's self-titled album went to number 76 on the charts. The single "It's Not You, It's Not Me" rose to sixth position on *Billboard*'s Album Rock Tracks, and "America" got to number 8 on the same chart.

Gaines has one footnote to the story. "This was when vinyl was still plentiful. Paul had this great idea for the inner spiral, where the record comes to an end and the needle keeps going around and around. He wanted to put a dog whistle sound on that part so it would attract attention from dogs while the record needle went around and around. I thought it was a great idea. Unfortunately, the record company was not impressed, and they nixed the idea."

CHAPTER 23

A New Owner at the Record Plant
1986

GAINES RETURNED to the Record Plant following its reopening after it was seized by the federal government, and one of the first projects he brought to the studio was a new record by Santana. The album they worked on at the time would be called *Freedom*. Unfortunately, the studio was still operating as a subsidiary of "Club Fed."

"After the studio was up and going again, the authorities put it up for auction," Gaines recalls. "I often wondered where the money went after the sale was completed. Several people who were interested in bidding on it called me to ask me what I thought it was worth, but more importantly, what I would do if and when it was sold. Several people were interested in buying it, including Ted Nugent. I talked to him and his manager about it several times, and I really thought he might be the one who would win the auction."

Gaines recalls that a young person representing the Zucker movie organization (responsible for the 1980 blockbuster comedy *Airplane* as well as the *Naked Gun* franchise) from Los Angeles also expressed interest. "I never talked to them directly, but I did speak to a broker attorney who represented them or the family. They seemed to really want the studio. Although they didn't win the bidding, they did call back and asked me if I would be interested in setting up a studio for them in Hawaii. The family owned a horse ranch on Kona, and it had guest houses that could accommodate the bands that would go there to record. They not only wanted American bands but also Japanese bands. Japanese tourists loved to vacation there, and while there, they could record as well. They pursued the idea for several months."

Almost all of those who were interested in buying the studio wanted to know what would happen to Gaines if they ended up being the owners; everyone, that is, except the person who did win. "He never contacted me," Gaines says.

The individual's name was Bob Skye. Hailing from the East Coast, Skye had a small remote studio truck business, but he had never owned a real studio. He eventually brought in a veteran engineer and producer from Los Angeles, Arne Frager, as his partner. Gaines assumed that the reason for that was to pull business in from Southern California.

"This also meant that I was back to being just another client of the studio," Gaines says. "Dealing with Bob Skye after the official transfer of ownership in 1987 was a distinctly different kind of relationship than I was used to. I don't think he had any idea how much business I had done there, or how much more I could do. He seemed more interested in how things worked in LA. He came in underfunded and needed a partner to help with the expenses. He had taken out some short-term bridge loans to get in, but the money to service those loans quickly ran out. That's why he needed a partner."

Before long, Skye was making changes that Gaines thought ill advised. "I remember one time, he changed the speaker system while I wasn't there. After listening to it, I told him to go back to the old system. It was all wrong. He didn't like that. Remember, his experience was with remote-truck recording, not an actual studio. He was determined to try new things that he had simply heard of or read about. Not surprisingly, we ended up having a few clashes."

On the other hand, Gaines found Arne Frager to be much more understanding. "He was a studio engineer and knew what I was talking about. Later on, Arne would end up as the sole owner."

As much as he had loved the Plant, Gaines discovered that its new ownership represented a drag on his career that he couldn't overcome. "I had brought in a lot of business to the Plant, but it seemed that none of my efforts were appreciated."

It was time for Gaines to move on.

Getting in the Groove with the Neville Brothers

1987

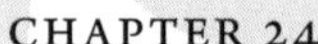

THE NEXT PROJECT INVOLVED the Neville Brothers from Louisiana, and Gaines couldn't have been more delighted. He considered them a great groove group and one of the funkiest bands he had ever heard. Based in New Orleans, they became international ambassadors for the state of Louisiana.

Although there were normally four brothers in the band—Art on keyboards, Cyril on percussion, Charles on sax, and Aaron doing the vocals—Charles wasn't able to participate during the initial sessions because of health problems. Later, Branford Marsalis was enlisted to do the sax parts.

After Gaines spoke with the group's management, they decided that he should fly to New Orleans and check out the local studios for recording possibilities. The brothers had worked at several studios in New Orleans, but there was one in particular that they didn't want to use: Sea-Saint—the studio belonging to Marshall Sehorn and Allen Toussaint.

"I guess some things had taken place in the past that were involved in that decision," Gaines says. After exploring the other possibilities, they chose a small studio in Metairie, which had been a video production studio. "It was fairly small for us, but still usable," Gaines recalls. "They had very little gear, so I had mine flown in. They wanted us there really badly.

"Before starting, I asked Art Neville to fly to San Francisco to stay with me so that we could go over songs and preproduction. I also wanted to demo a few songs that were new, as well as going over some new outside material."

Cory Lerios from the group Pablo Cruise had a small studio where they could do the demos. Gaines also wanted Lerios to play on a couple of the songs.

"A few weeks earlier, I had a songwriter waiting outside my control room door, wanting to meet me and pitch his song," Gaines remembers. "He had heard about me working on the Neville Brothers' album and he wanted to personally hand me his song. He was a writer from Jobete Publishing, which was connected with Motown. So I took his cassette so I could listen to it later. When I heard it, I thought it would be great for the project. In fact, I liked it so well that I called the publisher and asked if I could buy the master tape of the song. It had some cool parts on it, including a great strings arrangement. I bought the song so that I could overdub to it later. It wasn't that the Neville Brothers couldn't write their own material, but I thought that song would fit the style we were going for."

During these prerecording sessions in California, there was one night that Gaines remembers in particular. "While Art was staying with me, he called home one night to talk to his wife. She wasn't there and he was upset, especially when he learned that she was out on the bayou. After he hung up, he told me, 'When I get home, I'm going out to the bayou with my knife and I'm going to be 'Ramfro!'"—a reference to the movie *Rambo* and Art Neville's Afro hairdo. "I never forgot that nickname," Gaines says with a grin, "and every time I saw him, that's what I would call him."

000

The Nevilles' project was unusual because it involved two record companies, Rounder Records and EMI. Rounder was the original label, but EMI was the distribution partner. "Normally, there would be a deposit sent in to me and the studio," Gaines explains. "I hadn't received my portion, but I decided to go ahead and get it started."

Gaines was named executive producer of the project and was assigned to produce four of the songs. The other producers were two Englishmen, Clive Langer and Alan Winstanley, and Richie Zito, who was from LA. "Clive and Alan would get their choice of two songs, because they were thought to be the 'singles' guys. That would leave Richie and me with four songs each. Clive and Alan had good credentials, since they had just finished recording a Rolling Stones single. We decided that I would go first, then Clive and Alan, and last, Richie."

The band would initially consist of the brothers Art on keys and Cyril on percussion, augmented by Darryl Johnson on bass, Brian Stoltz on guitar, and

Willie Green on drums. Later, Branford Marsalis was added on sax, along with a variety of guitarists that included Keith Richards, Carlos Santana, Jerry Garcia, and Ronnie Montrose.

"When we first started tracking, I noticed that Art would be standing there listening one moment, and then all of sudden he would be asleep," Gaines says. "I asked him about it, and he explained to me that he had narcolepsy. I asked him if it was okay for him to drive, and he replied, 'Not really.' It turned out that he had wrecked his car a few times because he would nod off. I asked him about some of the other unusual things that had happened due to his disorder. He told me that one of his first jobs was as an elevator operator in a large department store, but he got fired after a few days because he would fall asleep between floors and end up taking his passengers to the basement.

"We had fun cutting the tracks, and in between, each of the guys would take turns making their version of gumbo. All of them were great. I asked Art what went into his gumbo, and he said, 'Anything and everything, from roadkill on up.' I had a hard time believing that, but it was really good."

Once Gaines was finished tracking his songs for the album, he suggested that instead of Aaron Neville singing the demo he had chosen, Cyril would be a better choice, because his voice fit the style better. He also decided to try incorporating some new sounds for the band, including a sitar, and using other keyboard programs that gave the music a more modern sound. And along the way, in between takes, he also had a great time listening to Art share some of his past adventures.

"There was the one he told me about when he and Aaron were going to LA on a bus. They had very little money, so they brought a bag of fried chicken with them to eat. Along the way they met two young ladies, and somehow the girls got to their chicken and ate it all. They were left with no food, which meant they were pretty hungry once they got to their destination."

000

About halfway through tracking, the studio approached Gaines and told him that they had never received their deposit for the sessions. They needed to get some money immediately, they said, or they would delay any further work. Gaines got on the phone and told the label to either get them some money or he himself would stop the session and take the tapes home with him. Apparently the technique worked, because the money showed up right away. "Sometimes you just have to threaten them," Gaines says.

Meanwhile, Gaines brought in his assistant Stephen Hart to help with the engineering. Hart was a great engineer, and later he became a very important part of the Bay Area recording scene. "Tracking went well, especially with the English guys," Gaines said. "They had to have their teatime in the afternoon, but I think there was more than tea in the cups.

"On our last day of tracking, Willie Green came in with a bandage on his leg. I asked if he was able to play drums, and he said he could. Then I asked him how he got injured, and he replied, 'I got shot in the leg riding my bike to 7-Eleven last night, but it was okay because it was only a .22 bullet.'"

Gaines says that working with the English guys was a lot of fun, and that he even picked up a couple of tricks from them in the process. He also enjoyed working with Branford Marsalis, even though the saxophonist hadn't slept in almost two days because of his touring schedule.

"Carlos came in at the very end and put a few parts down," Gaines recalls. "Richie Zito came in last to do his songs. He is a great producer, but I got the feeling that our little studio was somewhat below his normal professional standard. The English crew would take their songs back to England to finish. I took mine and a few of Richie's back to the Plant to put additional overdubs on. I sent a tape to Keith Richards for his parts. I also told my assistant Steve that when Jerry Garcia came in, he would be bringing a big amp setup. I had always seen him playing several large amps at once. So, wouldn't you know it, Jerry walks in with a cut-down Steinberger guitar and a briefcase-sized amp. I looked at him and said, 'Where the heck is the rest of your gear?' He laughed and said, 'I hate dealing with all that stuff.' Then he asked me what I wanted him to play. I said, 'Give me some great Jerry Garcia.' And he did.

"When it got to mixing, we mixed our parts of the project separately. The English mixes were great, but Richie's mixes were very bright compared to the rest of ours. I asked him if he was sure that was how he wanted it to sound, and ultimately we went with it. God bless the mastering guy!"

Gaines's demo song "Whatever It Takes," pitched to him by the songwriter at his studio door, ended up being the first single released from the album, which surprised him immensely.

"The album, titled *Uptown*, got some attention, but their next album would be even more successful. I was happy for them. Art Neville passed in 2019. May he rest in peace."

CHAPTER 25

A Holler from Hornsby

1988

AT THIS POINT, GAINES AND JOURNEY needed a new plan for completing an album that was still in progress. "After the [Plant] was shut down by the authorities, we had to change studios to finish recording," Gaines explains.

"First we went to Jonathan Cain's house. He had a small setup in an office where he could finish up his keyboards and a few guitar parts. Later we went to Fantasy to work on vocals and the rest of the guitar parts. Steve wanted to bring in Randy Goodrum, a friend of his from LA, to help him with his vocals. As a result, there were quite a few breaks during the recording time."

During one of those breaks, Gaines got a call asking him about working on Bruce Hornsby's new record. Hornsby had written the song "Jacob's Ladder," one of the hits on the *Fore!* album. "The original deal was that Huey and I would start Bruce's album together with three or four cuts, then I would finish it up by producing the rest of the album. So Huey and I went down to Rumbo Studios and started tracking with Bruce."

Gaines had met Bruce only once before, and that was because of his association with Huey Lewis's publishing activity. "I found him to be a very funny and talented guy, and he had a great band as well. As we were doing the tracking, he brought up an experience with Val Garay and his studio. So I told him about my encounters with Val. Bruce then decided that we ought to mess with him a little bit. Of course, that idea was right up my alley.

"Bruce came up with a great idea. He imitated the voice of a very southern-sounding construction manager and called Record One, asking to speak to Val's chief engineer. When the guy got on the phone, Bruce told him that he was apologizing for being late and that his crew was on the way to tear down the wall in their Studio A. He insisted that Val wanted it done today.

"Of course the rest of us were all listening to the conversation on a speaker phone. We could tell that this guy was going ballistic. He insisted that Val hadn't said anything to him about any of this. But Bruce was explaining that this was what Val wanted. The conversation continued for a few minutes, and meanwhile we were all dying laughing. Finally, Bruce told the guy that the crew would wait to come the next day, and he hung up."

000

With Huey Lewis, Gaines finished up the tracking for Hornsby's record and returned home. But because he was in the middle of recording the Journey album, he couldn't commit to finishing Bruce Hornsby's project.

"While working at Fantasy, we were doing vocals in the old Creedence Clearwater Studio C," Gaines recalls. "We didn't need the big room. But at Fantasy, the big room had lots of nice snacks, like coffee cake, fruit, and other goodies. The small room only provided a little fruit.

"They brought the Bruce Hornsby project up to mix in the big room while we were in the back. Steve Perry had recorded in that Studio D room on previous albums and he knew the routine there. So one day we ask Nina Bombardier, the studio manager, why we couldn't get coffee cake, and she explained that it was because the studio rate was different. I told the manager, Roy Seagle, that we needed coffee cake, too. Unfortunately, he said no."

The next morning Gaines went into Studio D and stole Hornsby's coffee cake and shared it with the crew working on the Journey album. "Roy came over and asked who stole the cake. Of course, it was pretty obvious it was us, because there we were finishing it. Steve and I told him, 'You might want to make sure that we get some coffee cake every morning. Otherwise, you can guess what's going to happen.' We got coffee cake from then on."

After the vocals were finished, the tapes went to Bob Clearmountain for mixing. This was done mostly at Bearsville Studios, just west of Woodstock, New York, with a bit done at the Power Station, a studio in New York City's Hell's Kitchen.

"After Steve, Jonathan, and Neal came back from the mixing session, I asked how it went and what was it like up there. Neal didn't like it; he said that the place was haunted. They were staying in some cabins and, according to Neal, there were strange noises every night outside his room. He was ready to get the heck out of there. I have worked in several studios that I was pretty sure were haunted, and I have my own stories. But that particular studio does have a reputation." Interestingly, the musician Meat Loaf has also been known to tell similar tales about Bearsville.

Ultimately, the album, *Raised on Radio*, went platinum, although it was less successful than Journey's previous offering. The Hornsby album that Gaines helped with, *The Way It Is*, went platinum as well. Gaines says that in his opinion, they're both great albums.

000

Gaines's next project brought him back to Fantasy Studios. "During the time the Plant was closed, Roy Seagle asked if I would consider working out of Fantasy," he says. "I gave it a try, but it wasn't the same feel that I experienced before. All the people were very nice and they did have good facilities, but the studio also had a very corporate vibe."

Gaines worked on a project by a young band from Sacramento called Steel Breeze. A hard rock band, they had had some success with their previous album. Kim Fowley, their most recent producer, wasn't involved in their latest album, and Gaines wasn't even sure who was in charge.

"The lead singer, Ric Jacobs, had one of the most unusual vocal warmup routines I had ever heard. When I first heard him in the studio, I wondered what was going on out there. It sounded like a cross between a monk's chant and a half scream. I actually thought someone had gotten hurt.

"I also remember that one of the guitarists was really into the *Mad Max* movie that had recently come out. As a result, we rented the video of the movie and screened it in the control room whenever he was doing his overdubs. I got to see that movie a lot. But sometimes you have to do whatever it takes to get the track."

The band also brought in Clarence Clemons from Bruce Springsteen's E Street Band to do some sax parts on the album, although, Gaines says, "I'm not sure why, because the band didn't normally use a sax player. It was my first time working with Clarence. He was a big guy and he played sax like no one I had ever heard before. His sound came across like he was playing through a Marshall amp, loud and distorted."

Later, at the Plant, Gaines would work on an album of Clemons's that Narada Michael Walden was producing. Titled *Hero*, the album was released not long after Springsteen's popular *Born in the USA* album, and it contained two hit singles, "You're a Friend of Mine" and "I Wanna Be Your Hero."

"I have to say that Narada Michael Walden was one of nicest people that I've ever known in the business," Gaines says, "and he's a great drummer and producer as well. I remember him getting his start in producing at the Automatt. I'm very glad that I got to work with him. He later acquired his own studio in San Rafael, and he recorded a lot of big hits from there."

Gaines ended up doing a couple of small projects before ending that particular stint at Fantasy. Nevertheless, he would return later to do several Santana albums at that studio.

CHAPTER 26

Working with Melissa Etheridge
1988

WHILE GAINES WAS STILL at the Plant, he received a call from Melissa Etheridge's manager about the possibility of working with her. She had just signed with Chris Blackwell's Island Records and was looking to record a new album.

"I flew down to LA and arranged with her manager to meet her at a small club so I could watch her perform," he recalls. "She was doing a solo acoustic act at that particular time. I thought her songs were great, that they were different, and it was obvious that she could belt them out."

Her A&R representative at the label, Rob Fraboni, wanted to produce the album himself, but Etheridge and her manager wanted someone else to do it. "Fraboni was very plugged into the New York scene and had people like Keith Richards staying over at his house at various times," Gaines says. "So he ended up being my contact at the record company. Of course that involved another political situation, since he had wanted to produce the album. As a result, I requested him to be there during the mixes, hoping he would give his okay to everything that occurred during the recordings. I was trying to protect myself from whatever might transpire in the future. In fact, it was the only time in my career that I had to put that in my contract."

Etheridge wanted to choose the musicians in the band. They were all based in Los Angeles, and some were members of Bonnie Raitt's group. "At that point, I always had a day or two for rehearsals before we would begin recording," Gaines says. "So we rehearsed in LA and then moved to the Plant to record. I had Cory Lerios from Pablo Cruise join us to play some keyboard parts. I wanted to make the songs rock a little more as opposed to keeping a strictly acoustic feel."

During the sessions, Gaines says that he and Etheridge went out to clubs at night after the day's recording was done. "We'd end up checking out all the same girls. I had never experienced anything like that before! She was a lot of fun to hang out with."

At the same time, Gaines was using their social interactions to make sure Etheridge approved of the way the sessions were proceeding. "She said she was happy with things, and that was great with me. I've never seen myself as a producer who has to have it my way. Instead, I look at my role as trying to help the artist make the record that they want to make."

In this case, the session musicians were accomplished and their style meshed well with Etheridge's. "When we finished the tracks, we moved the sessions to LA so she could be home and feel more relaxed when it came time for her to do the vocals. We were working in a studio owned by a couple of Armenians who kept a close eye on everything that took place in the building. For example, the coffee machine was located in a small room just off the street. One day, I went to get some and I discovered that the machine had just been stolen. So I went to the owner and tried to explain what happened. He said to me, 'That's it! I'm not getting another one! You guys will have to go down the street to the 7-Eleven and get coffee.' So that's what we did."

The vocal sessions went smoothly, and Etheridge was singing well. "Actually, she could sing like crazy," Gaines says. "But I had another interesting experience during the sessions. Melissa lived with her partner, a woman who was a little older. She would come by the studio after she got off work and hang out for part of the evening.

"However, Melissa also had a younger woman that she was seeing as well, who would come by in the early afternoon. That was to ensure that there would be no overlap in their visits. The problem was that the younger one drank a certain kind of water, and one day she left a bottle in the control room. When Melissa's roommate showed up, she saw the water and immediately recognized who brought it in there. She started in on Melissa, and suddenly we had a little catfight going on. Eventually things settled down and we went back to work. But that was a first for me."

Gaines also recalls that a particular photographer was hired to take some studio shots during the recording sessions. "The problem was, this guy was a jerk as well as a chauvinist. He was condescending to Melissa and to her partner. Plus he pissed me off, and it upset my sessions. I called the manager and told him to get the guy out and find someone else to take the pictures. Sometimes it was good having a little power so I could control my sessions."

When the instrumental tracks were sufficiently completed, Gaines played them for Rob Fraboni, who approved them before Etheridge began recording the vocals. "While we were doing the vocals, the president of the label, Chris Blackwell, who had personally signed Melissa, came by to visit and listen to what we had down so far. He seemed okay with what he heard. He certainly appeared to be happy with the progress.

"But when it came time to mix, Rob Fraboni called and asked if I would go down to Compass Point, their studio in the Bahamas, to do the mixing. I said I would rather not, because if I needed any guitar parts, the player was only an hour away from where we were at the moment. To me, that made more sense than having to fly someone down to the Bahamas. He persisted, but I kept declining. Later, I found out that the real reason he wanted us there was because he got a percentage of all the business he brought into the studio. Nevertheless, he came to the studio and gave us his opinions on the mix. I didn't agree with some of it, but I did try to use some of his ideas."

After finishing the mixes, Gaines sent them to the president of the label for US operations, who was based in New York. "He called back and told me he loved the rock feel of the record. Then two weeks later, I got a call from the manager saying Chris Blackwell thought it rocked too much and he wanted it more like the young lady I heard in that small club playing acoustically. He wanted to recut everything with just the band."

Blackwell is known for turning the world on to reggae and boosting the careers of artists like Bob Marley, U2, Grace Jones, and the B-52s. "Obviously, I have huge respect for Chris," Gaines says, "but—wow! This was very unexpected, especially since he had okayed everything earlier in LA and had said he liked what he heard."

Ultimately the record company would keep all of Gaines's arrangements and recut the tracks, with Kevin McCormick, the bass player, as the album's producer. "This was only one of two projects I've done that didn't come out as planned," Gaines says. The other, he relates, happened later when the label he was recording for fired the artist and repertoire person and shelved the three projects she had signed, including the one Gaines was working on at the time.

Such outcomes were certainly infrequent in Jim Gaines's career, but on this occasion the experience left him ready to move on. And he would not have to wait long for the opportunity.

Dueling Doobies

1988

"THE DOOBIE BROTHERS have always been one of my favorite bands," Gaines claims. "When I was at Heider's, I got a chance to work with them on some of their last demos before they got signed with Warner Bros. Records. Bruce and Marty Cohen were involved in those sessions; Marty ended up working for Warner Brothers, and Bruce ended up as their manager.

"I had worked with Tommy Johnston"—lead guitarist, singer, and songwriter for the Doobies—"on some of his demos after he left the band. Some of the band hung out at the Plant at various times. They were all from the San Jose area. And all of them were biker types. I remember 'Big John' Hartman [the band's original drummer] used to pull his motorcycle into the studio so it wouldn't get stolen."

Gaines was hired as the engineer for the sessions. There were two producers: Charlie Midnight, the writer and producer; and Eddie Schwartz, described by Gaines as "a guy from Canada that I thought had likely never produced anything before." Gaines recalled that Charlie Midnight had written some songs for Joe Cocker's *Unchain My Heart* album the previous year. Midnight also wrote the 1987 Grammy-nominated song "Living in America," recorded by James Brown.

The Doobie Brothers had gone through several iterations since they first formed. By 1988, Michael McDonald, who joined the group as keyboardist and vocalist in 1975, had left the band, and Tommy Johnston was the front man once again. The band was using two drummers, John Hartman and Mike Hossack. Tiran Porter was on bass, Pat Simmons played guitar, and Bobby LaKind covered auxiliary percussion. Johnston sang and played guitar.

"I'm used to running a fairly tight and quick session, but this one was disjointed from the start," Gaines notes. "The band had been in rehearsal with the producers for a couple of weeks, but things still felt very loose. Eddie Schwartz had just started using computer technology to record and had used it to record part of a rehearsal."

Schwartz was mainly a guitar player and songwriter, Gaines remembers. "He was not easy to work with, mainly because he had no idea how to use the recording techniques that we were working with at that time. His personality made him difficult as well. Still, Charlie let him run the session while he sat on the sofa, reading the paper and working on puzzles."

Mike Hossack was the only drummer used during the studio tracking sessions, but Gaines recalls that John Hartman was in the studio as well. "Eddie had me sync up our tape machine to his computer so he could try switching drum parts [between Hossack and Hartman] as we went along. It was a nightmare. He somehow changed some of the parts around and created a real mess while we were doing overdubs."

The resulting confusion led to an argument between the two drummers about parts being changed, and unfortunately, this was not the only interpersonal friction during the project. "I had just hired a young lady named Devon Beradoni as my assistant engineer," Gaines says. "She had some great credits and experience. She had an easygoing, laid-back attitude but still managed to stay right on top of things. Still, for some reason, Eddie didn't like her, or maybe it was because he had never worked with a female engineer before. There was always some tension there, and I had to put him in his place several times."

Gaines recalls that it took longer than it should have just to get three tracks partially done. "It was going really slow with all these experiments going on," he says.

"One day, we finally get around to trying out Tiran on bass parts," he said. "As I was playing the song, Tiran was playing along. But Eddie was bringing up different kick drum parts as the track continued, which made it impossible for Tiran to lock into the track, since bass players play off the kick groove. I finally told Eddie that it was totally wrong. Meanwhile, Charlie was letting the situation go on as he sat on the couch, reading the paper.

Eventually, the situation developed into a confrontation between Gaines and Schwartz. "As the session engineer, I'm supposed to go with the flow, but given my experience as a producer, I also knew that this was a bullshit situation."

When they were preparing to record Pat Simmons's guitar parts, Gaines received a request to hook up a second tape machine and lock them together to make more tracks available. "We did this a lot, but we still had empty tracks left on the first machine," Gaines says. "Eddie had heard of this technique but had never used it. I told him we didn't need to do that yet, since we still had open tracks on the first machine. But he was adamant, so we did what he wanted, and sure enough, it became another waste of time and energy."

At this point, they were four weeks into the project and had only three tracks in progress. That was unheard of as far as Gaines was concerned. "I called the band's manager and told him that he needed to look at what was going on here, since we were already about one hundred thousand dollars into the budget."

To make matters worse, the problems between Schwartz and Gaines's assistant, Devon Beradoni, had only gotten worse. "Devon ended up having a partial breakdown; she actually had to go to the doctor over it.

"As much as I wanted to work on this record, things were simply going wrong. So, I pulled Tommy Johnston aside and told him that I might have to leave the project. He wasn't blind, of course; he could see what was happening. He had a power meeting with the producers and told them that if I left, he would go as well, even though I insisted that he shouldn't do that."

After that confrontation, the producers went to Gaines and asked him to stay. He had also told the band's management what was going on and that they ought to be aware that the sessions were out of control.

"We finally got to the vocals, and that's when Charlie Midnight got up off the sofa and got involved," Gaines explains. "I guess that was what he was waiting for."

Even so, after another week or so, they still had only three tracks down. With more crazy things going on, Gaines reluctantly decided he had to leave. "I gave my notice to Tommy first, apologizing for bailing out on him. I was really torn. I told the manager I would leave, but not until they had someone to replace me. They brought someone in a few days later, and soon after that, they fired the producers." They ended up using Rodney Mills, a producer from Atlanta with more than fifty gold and platinum albums to his credit. "They subsequently cut the whole album in about six weeks, which we should have been able to do in the first place," Gaines says.

The album would be called *Cycles*. One of the songs Gaines recorded was "The Doctor," which became the band's final hit single. It reached the number 1 spot on the *Billboard* rock charts and peaked at number 9 on the *Billboard* Hot 100.

"That project was a real disappointment to me personally, but I still love those Doobies," Gaines says in retrospect.

After that effort, Gaines worked on a few smaller projects that turned out to be some of his final work at the Plant while he lived in Marin County. He would eventually end up back in Memphis, even though he did come back to the Bay Area and work on some other albums there later.

CHAPTER 28

Farewell to Frisco

1988

BEFORE GAINES COULD LEAVE the Plant and the city by the bay, he had a few final projects to finish up. One involved recording some songs for a film titled *Fool for Love.* It was a Sam Shepard play that had been made into a movie directed by Robert Altman, starring Sam Shepard, Kim Basinger, and Harry Dean Stanton. The music was written and performed by Shepard's sister, Sandy Rogers.

Gaines asked to read the script so he would have some idea what the music should sound like for each of the scenes it was meant for. "I had spoken with Robert Altman while he was editing the film in Paris, and he mentioned that he would get me one," Gaines insists. "Unfortunately, I never got it, so there we were, doing songs for a scene in which I had no idea what was supposed to be happening.

"Sandy was a great singer and had a kind of country and folk feel to her songs. Understandably, she was a little nervous because she had never done anything like this before. I suggested that we should just do the best we could, even though we weren't sure exactly where in the film the music would be used. We also didn't know that one of the songs would be placed at the opening of the movie. She knew that the first scene would show a truck driving over a hill into a small town, where it would end up at a motel. The motel was supposedly where most of the story would take place."

Gaines took the song that he and the singer believed might fit best with the initial scene and then shaped it into an arrangement that they thought would work best with both the visuals and the timing needed. "We approached some of the other songs more like typical album cuts," Gaines explains. "It was fun to work with Sandy, and it was easy to get her performing in the style and feel she was known for. I also had a couple of conversations with Robert Altman and then played him what we thought would fit the movie's opening sequence. He said he was pleased with what we played him over the phone. At that point, it didn't take us very long to finish and send everything to Altman. He said it was all great, and that it would work well for the movie. I think we ended up doing seven songs in total."

At the film's premiere, Gaines was accompanied by a lady friend, he says. "We had dinner and drinks before going to the movie. I guess that between that and being really tired, I fell asleep during the credits. I never did get to see my name on the big screen. I also didn't feel right about asking that lady out again, since I probably seemed like kind of a dud. So much for a potential relationship and also my movie career." Later, however, Gaines would have better luck.

000

One of Gaines's most unusual experiences occurred just before he left the West Coast. It involved a young man who called him several times, asking Gaines to help him do some demos.

"At the time I wasn't really doing this type of thing," he says. "Even after agreeing to do it, I wasn't comfortable with the band he had chosen, because it wasn't what we had talked about. Then, when we began recording, I saw he was really wound up. I didn't think it was a natural high, either. Later, I found out that it wasn't. Not only couldn't he play well, he was also really nervous and definitely not focused.

"Consequently, after a couple of hours, I told him that it wasn't working. He started crying and apologizing for his condition. I suggested that he needed to stop and try again some other time. He was devastated, but I sent him home anyway. Later, he called me and asked if I would work with him again, and I told him that I didn't think that was a good idea.

"Then, a couple of weeks later, I got a letter from him. The letter was packaged with a cassette that had what looked like blood on it. Sure enough, the note said, 'I'm giving you everything, including my blood, just to work with you again.'"

To say the least, this communication did nothing to increase Gaines's comfort level for working with this particular aspiring artist. But even that wasn't the end of the story.

"The guy stalked me for several years. He even found me later while I was in Europe, working with a French group in Paris. Out of the blue, I got a call from him. There weren't too many people who knew where I was working, and I still don't know how he found out where I was. He told me he was in an institution, that he had broken into the office, and that he was talking to me while hiding under a desk."

Gaines observes that while it's nice to be wanted, he didn't really need someone as a client who gave every evidence of being a walking mental time bomb. Eventually, the young man's calls and messages ceased, but not until providing some moments of serious concern for Gaines.

Happily, though, he was about to segue from the weird to the wonderful. A guitar player named Stevie Ray Vaughan was waiting in the wings.

CHAPTER 29

Stevie Ray Vaughan and Double Trouble

1989

IN LATE 1988, GAINEs got a call from Stevie Ray Vaughan's manager, Alex Hodges, asking whether he would be interested in working with Vaughan and his band Double Trouble on a new project. Gaines thought that working with Vaughan would be an honor because he was considered one of the finest guitar players in the world at the time. They asked him to fly to LA to meet the band.

"We met at the Sunset Marquis hotel," Gaines remembers. "After I met everyone, one of the first questions Stevie asked was how I would feel about recording with ten amps at once. I told him it would be kind of an engineering nightmare. I had recorded Ronnie Montrose with six, and with Santana we did four or five sometimes. I told him I thought it would be a pretty tough challenge."

As it turned out, Carlos Santana had recommended Gaines to Vaughan when the two guitarists were doing a show together. That had resulted in the present meeting, even though Gaines was aware that they were looking at several other producers.

"About three weeks later, I was in Canada working when I got a call from the A&R guy at Epic Records. The conversation started like this: 'Well, Jim, you weren't my choice, but the band chose you to do the album.'

"He was going to be my new label boss, so I wasn't sure how to respond. I would have to answer to him during the recording and production, and yet I now knew I wasn't the guy he wanted. Not the ideal way to go into a project."

When Gaines got home later, Hodges, the band's manager, called and told him, "Don't talk to the label. We don't like them, and if you do, you will be fired."

"Now I'm thinking, 'Great! I'm caught in another political power struggle,'" Gaines says. Not permitted to communicate with representatives of the record label, Gaines was also in the position of needing to get approval for arrangements and expenses from someone who didn't want to be working with him. Still, after agreeing on a recording schedule and location with the band, Gaines thought they were ready to get started.

Unfortunately, it wouldn't be so easy.

"The A&R guy from the label called me and said he wanted to know what songs we would be recording," Gaines remembers. "He also wanted to go over the budget. First he told me that the band had submitted a budget of two hundred fifty thousand dollars. I almost fell out of my chair when he said that. This was a four-piece Texas blues band, and the larger the budget, the longer it takes to recoup before anyone gets any royalties. I figured that the budget should have been around one hundred thousand. However, the label guy said he would approve it, because the band had recouped the advances on their other albums.

"After listening to him for a while, I said, 'Mike, I can't talk to you about any of this, because the band prohibits me from talking to you.' Naturally, that didn't go over very well.

"About an hour later I got a call from Alex Hodges, telling me that the label had just called him and said that I had spoken with them. I got warned again not to talk to the label, or else. Talk about being 'Caught in the Crossfire,' right?"

Someone had suggested that Gaines and the group try Butch Trucks's new studio in Tallahassee, Florida. Trucks was one of the drummers for the Allman Brothers Band, and he had just opened the facility. Gaines and Double Trouble would be only the second clients to record there. "Stevie, drummer Chris Layton, and I flew down to check it out. It was a beautiful studio, but it was very new and untested. We felt like we would be guinea pigs, and we really didn't want to be in that position."

Gaines believes that one of the reasons he was chosen for the project was that Stevie and the band had all quit doing drugs, drinking alcohol, and smoking. They didn't want anyone around them who would be a temptation. Since Gaines had never gotten into drugs, he believed that was part of the reason he was hired.

"After going and checking out the studio, we had dinner and retired to our rooms," Gaines explains. "After a while, I decided to go to the bar and have a late-night cocktail. I had just ordered my drink and as it was being delivered, I get a tap on my shoulder and there's Stevie standing behind me. I didn't know what to say except, 'I'm sorry, man. I ordered a drink.' He laughed and said, 'It's okay. Can I get a juice with you?' I didn't know what to do but to sit with him and enjoy our time together."

The band had been rehearsing in Texas, but Gaines wasn't asked to join them. It was decided that they would rehearse again in New York with Gaines before they all went into the studio. The Power Station, in midtown Manhattan, was ultimately chosen as the place where they would record. They booked four to six weeks.

"After rehearsal, we moved into the studio," Gaines explains. "We had been given a fairly small room to record in, and it had a small, pretty dead isolation booth for the amps. It was hard to even get all ten amps in there, much less get any kind of room sound with it. So we struggled to get going with guitar sounds, and eventually Stevie became frustrated with the way it was going.

"We tried what we could for three or four days. In the meantime, with that many amps going, I realized that I really needed more tracks for the initial tracking."

There was a 24-track analog tape machine as well as a 32-track digital machine in the building, so Gaines asked the band whether they would allow him to run a test on the 24-to-32 difference in sound, hoping that the result would enable him to utilize the extra tracks. They agreed. "So I had both machines set up at the same time and decided that I would record on them both and then do the playback with a switch that would go back and forth between the two. They wouldn't know which was being played. I had also brought in some old tube gear to help the digital sound get closer to the analog."

Vaughan and the band recorded a song for Gaines, and he had them listen to the playback. They couldn't tell the difference, so he was able to use the digital machine. "However, we still had this problem of amp sounds in this small room. I told Stevie that I had worked in a studio in Memphis that had a big tracking room and very large isolation booth, and that might work for us. I had recorded a band from Canada there a few months earlier."

The place was called Kiva Studios (later House of Blues), and it was owned by Gary Belz. Gaines called him, explained the situation, and asked whether, if they came, they could get some free time so they could decide whether to record there.

"Gary said anything we wanted was okay with him. After I told Stevie that, we agreed to give it a try. The building had two studios next to each other, so I asked Gary if I could rent both of them. That way I could use the other space for Stevie's guitar tech, Rene Martinez, to work on the guitars and we could also put some of the smaller amps in there. It would also give us control of the entire building. It ended up costing us only half of what the Power Station was going to cost me.

"Also, Gary's family owned the famous Hotel Peabody, and they gave us incredible rates, which saved me even more. When we left the New York studio, we still had lots of time booked, so that meant that canceling was going to be a problem. They ended up wanting to sue us, but CBS stepped in and told them if they did, they would pull all their artists out of there. That ended that."

Gaines went to Memphis ahead of the band to prep the studio situation, while Stevie Ray and Double Trouble went to Washington, DC, to play for the inauguration of President George W. Bush.

"I remembered that I had run into some unusual hum problems while I was at Kiva before, so I wanted to resolve those issues before the band arrived," Gaines continues. "I did several tests and even had the local studio techs helping me to try finding a solution. It wasn't a normal hum; something else was obviously going on. I even had the power company do some tests that included shutting down a local grid for ten minutes to help determine what was going on. If the people who lived in the neighborhood knew what I had done, they definitely wouldn't have been happy with me. When I finally called a friend of mine in New York and explained what was happening, he told me that the room had to be wrapped in copper. Of course, I said that wasn't going to happen."

After the band arrived, following their engagement at the inauguration, Gaines tried some other tests. With ten amps, including two tube screamers hooked together, the hum was even louder. In desperation, Gaines tried one more thing.

"I had suspected that our problem was something coming into the building. So I went out and bought some electric conduit and chicken wire. I built a contraption that looked like a baseball batting cage. It had three covered sides and the front was open. I had Stevie back into it, and fortunately it worked well enough for us to start recording. It knocked down the hum by a good seventy percent."

Subsequently, Gaines became known as "the crazy man who put Stevie Ray Vaughan in a chicken coop." He says the story has come up several times in the years since.

"Still, it was so loud in the amp room that I had to tape up all the light fixtures and even pull some wooden panels off the wall and then stuff them with foam," Gaines says. Even as the recording began, Vaughan was blowing up amps so often that Gaines turned to Bob Dylan's guitar tech, César Díaz, asking him to come in and try to repair the amps.

"César had brought along his prized Fender Bassman amp for Stevie to try. But little did he know how loud Stevie played. There were several conversations about getting the volume down. Finally, César just packed it in."

Fortunately, a solution was at hand. "As we were trying out different guitars, Stevie borrowed a guitar from someone and asked Rene to take off the neck and replace it with one of his. Naturally, I was really nervous about that, because I was sure the owner wouldn't approve. But ultimately, it all worked out."

For the sake of authenticity, Vaughan wanted to try to capture his guitar solos as the tracks were being laid down with the rest of the band. This method requires more time and typically many more takes, since the rest of the ensemble must nail their parts at the same time. Nevertheless, that was how tracking proceeded on the album.

"And of course, I would sometimes say that certain cuts weren't good enough," Gaines remembers. "Stevie was also trying different guitars on the various songs. Some worked and some didn't. People were also sending in songs for us to consider, and we actually tried a few of those."

While all this was taking place, a "royal" visitor would arrive at the studio. This, too, would cause certain delays in an already-extended recording process.

CHAPTER 30

A King Comes Calling

1989

AS GAINES WAS BUSILY involved with tracking sessions with Stevie Ray Vaughan, Albert King dropped by, simply to hang out. King, one of the all-time greats of blues guitar, was a lifelong idol for Vaughan, who had cut his musical teeth in the blues clubs of Oak Cliff, a majority-Black neighborhood in Dallas. "Stevie loved him," Gaines insists. "It also needs to be noted that Albert didn't mind telling you what was on his mind, anytime. I know that, because I knew him briefly while I was working at Stax back in the day.

"So there he was, sitting next to me at the console listening in, and right in the middle of the take he said, 'Jim, stop the tape. I want to talk to Mister Hi Hat Man,' which is what he called the drummer. King went into the studio and proceeded to tell Chris Layton how he should be playing the song. Chris looked at Stevie and me for some help, but I couldn't say anything. As I said, Albert was a very strong-willed person.

"Later on, I got a call from the front desk, saying that Bon Jovi was in town doing a show, and Jon wanted to know if Stevie and Albert wanted to come over and sit in. I got on the talk-back, with Albert sitting next to me, and I asked both of them if they wanted to join Bon Jovi that night. Albert turned to me and said, 'Hey, Jim, them Bon Jovis, are they big?' I said, 'Yes, they are pretty big.' It apparently didn't matter, because he ended up playing cards that night. I had to call the front office and get someone to take him to lunch so we could get back to working."

As an aside, Gaines mentions that his wife, Sandy, cowrote a song that Albert King recorded on what was to be his last album. "She's very proud of that," he says.

"Later, when I was recording an album for the Kinsey Report group, I had my last encounter with Albert. Donald Kinsey and Albert were friends, and the Kinsey brothers were going to do a show at B. B. King's place on Beale Street while they were doing the recording. Albert was going to sit in and hang out during the show. The day of the gig, John Wooler from Virgin Records found out from Donald about Albert guesting with the band. So John called me and asked if I was going to go to the gig that night, and I said I was. He told me to make Albert an offer to sign with Virgin to make a record, with me producing."

The night of the show, Gaines was sitting with Albert King and Donald Kinsey, and when they took a break, Gaines said to Albert, "Virgin wants to offer you a record deal, and if you agree, they will put thirty thousand dollars in your pocket and the two of us will coproduce it right here in Memphis."

Gaines says, "Albert looked at me and said, 'Jim, I don't trust any of them SOBs. I don't think I want to do it.' Now at that point, he hadn't made a record in a very long time. The sad part is that he died not too long after that. It would have been his last record, and I would have given anything to be the producer."

000

"There were times when we were tracking Stevie Ray Vaughan," Gaines says, "that he wanted to talk to Janna [Lapidus LeBlanc, his girlfriend], and she wasn't reachable. She was working in New York but wasn't always available to talk. Sometimes when Stevie was in waiting mode, he would simply go out and play by himself. He would get into a Jimi Hendrix mode, and you would swear that Hendrix was in the building. Stevie would just be out there and he would get into certain moods where he would play the most amazing stuff. I tried to record some of it, but I don't know whatever happened to the recordings. Meanwhile, the band would be forced to sit and wait around, and some of the guys complained to me. They'd say, 'Jim, go out there and tell him we need to work.' I'd say, 'Hey, he's your bandmate. You tell him. I'm not going out there. I'm enjoying it.'"

One of the more interesting songs Gaines recorded for Vaughan and Double Trouble was an instrumental, "Riviera Paradise." Vaughan had told Gaines that he had this "little instrumental," and there was no need to rehearse. "When it came time to record, I usually wanted to track these types of songs at night with the lights down in the studio and in the control room; it made for good atmosphere. So, before we started, I asked Stevie how long the song would be. He said, 'Oh it's pretty short.' I had about eight minutes of tape left on the machine, and I thought I'd have enough for at least one take, if not two.

"The band started playing and it was sounding really good, but the tune kept going longer. I looked at my tape counter and realized that we might run out of tape before the end of the track. Meanwhile, Stevie had his back to me, the studio was dark, and I was starting to freak out. I was running around the control room trying to get someone's attention, when finally Chris Layton looked up at me. I was giving him hand signals to tell him that the tape was running out and he needed to end the song. Stevie happened to look at Chris, and he got the sign to stop. I swear, it ended with just a few seconds left on the tape. Ultimately, it was a beautiful take. We tried it again later but couldn't beat that original take. The only thing we ended up adding was a big rain stick at the end that someone had given Stevie, and it worked out great. The song ended up being almost eight minutes long. Even now, it's one of my favorite tracks. Later, the record company tried cutting it down for radio. They called me to do the edit, but neither of us could cut it and still keep the right feeling. What a great song!"

Speaking of one of the album's most well-known cuts, "Crossfire," Gaines says, "I wanted to do it in a way that would have some real radio appeal. It must have worked, because we got lots of airplay." Indeed they did: "Crossfire" became Vaughan's only number 1 hit, reaching the top position on *Billboard*'s Mainstream Rock list.

"We held off doing 'Life by the Drop' until we got to LA to do the mixing and vocals. It was an acoustic guitar and vocal cut." Ultimately, "Life by the Drop" and "Boot Hill" would end up on Vaughan's *The Sky Is Crying* album, a combination of several cuts that were left over from earlier albums.

Gaines recalls that Vaughan had evidently talked to guitarist Eric Johnson about some of his recording techniques. Johnson, who is probably best known for his 1992 Grammy-winning instrumental "Cliffs of Dover," was a proponent of a particular type of cable from RadioShack that had arrows printed on it, supposedly pointing in the direction the electrons ran. "He told Stevie they would give him a better sound. Mind you, these cables were only about five feet long and very impractical with our big setup. What's more, I would defy anyone to tell me that they could hear the difference. Still, this was one more distraction to deal with, not to mention that there are miles of cable in every studio, and none of them run in any certain direction. It's no wonder that Eric takes so long to make an album," Gaines opines.

"A few years later I got a call from Eric Johnson's manager, Joe Priesnitz," Gaines recalls, "asking me if I would be interested in working with him. He had his own studio, and as a result he had plenty of time to work. I told him, 'Joe, you know I do records in five weeks, not five years.' He said, 'Well, that's why we want you.' So I ended up going to Austin and working there for a week. The first thing that happened when I got there was that the band pulled me aside and pleaded with me to get Eric to keep what we were going to do. It seemed that he kept recutting the same songs over and over. We ended up cutting about six songs, which he was going to finish later. Frankly, I don't think the album ever was finished."

While he was in the middle of tracking the Stevie Ray Vaughan sessions, Gaines got the flu. "Gary Belz, the studio owner, said, 'I'm going to set you up with a doctor,'" Gaines recalls. "So I went to his office, and who is it but the famous Dr. Nick, Elvis Presley's doctor. As I was going to the exam room, I could see Jerry Lee Lewis in the next room. Dr. Nick had gotten a bad rap for freely prescribing pills, but my experience was fine. He gave me some meds and called me on a Sunday morning to check on me; no other doctor had ever done that. He even called one more time to check on me again. So all in all, my experience with Dr. Nick was really good."

When Gaines and Double Trouble finished tracking in Memphis, Vaughan wanted to go to Los Angeles to record vocals and do final mixing. "Once we got there, we ended up using several different studios. We brought in Dave McNair to help us with the mix." McNair, a longtime industry professional, has worked with artists as diverse as Patti Smith, Cyndi Lauper, Rodney Crowell, Los Lobos, and Smash Mouth.

"Dave knew the guys from Austin, but doing the vocals took a little bit of time. Stevie didn't like the sound of his voice and he was a little insecure when he was singing. For every song we did, I had to get every kind of Halls cough drops they made. Plus I kept tea and honey on hand, and sometimes I'd put some lemon on a table for him when he was in the studio.

"He would pace the control room for a while before going out to sing. I pushed him to try and get better at performing his vocals. I'm sure that nobody had ever pushed him that hard before. He told me that was the hardest he had ever worked on his singing. Sure enough, the critics would say later that it was his best recorded singing performances." Unfortunately, however, Gaines recalls, some of the tracks were never finished because Vaughan had problems getting his vocal parts done.

In addition to recording "Life by the Drop," featuring just Vaughan and his guitar, they also put the Mexicali Horns on a couple of cuts for the album. "While we were there, Bruce Willis was hanging out with us," Gaines says. "He was married to Demi Moore at that time. I kidded around with him a little and asked him if she had given him permission to hang with the boys. He laughed and said yes. Of course, he's a harp player, so he loved being around other blues musicians."

While they were in Los Angeles, Gaines recalls that Stevie Ray's brother Jimmie spent time visiting the studio as well. "He and Stevie were trying to get their brother relationship back on track. I believe they had gotten to the point where they weren't talking. Nevertheless, they came up with the idea of doing a record together and not using either of their bands, thinking it would be less political that way. That's how the concept for the album *Family Style* was born."

Gaines and Dave McNair finished the mixes for the album about a week after the tracking was complete. It was eventually titled *In Step*, and it was in fact a big new step in both Vaughan's and Gaines's lives and careers. The album was also a big success in terms of both sales and airplay, going on to win a Grammy.

"While we were mixing, *Guitar Player* magazine sent a writer over to interview Stevie and me in the control room," Gaines recalls. "We were answering questions and talking about the making of the record. Then, around three weeks later, I got a call from Stevie's publicist. He was clearly upset, telling me that in the article, the writer gave the producer credit to Terry Manning." Manning, who had also worked at Stax Records, has produced albums for the likes of ZZ Top, Iron Maiden, Led Zeppelin, Bryan Adams, and many others.

"I couldn't believe it," Gaines continues. "I had sat right there with the guy for two hours. The PR guy said that the article was printed and about to come out, and there was nothing he could do. He eventually had the publisher of the magazine call me and apologize. The people at *Guitar Player* said it was too late to change the story, but they did promise me a special interview to make up for the mistake. After that, I quit doing interviews for many years.

I don't trust many writers because of that situation. And unfortunately, that wasn't the first time this type of thing had happened. Going forward, I decided to approve anything that I've supposedly said before the article goes to print.

"By the way," Gaines says with a smile, "I did get a call from Terry Manning after the article came out, and he thanked me for the nice credit."

000

On August 27, 1990, a little over a year after the release of *In Step*, Gaines was working in Lake Geneva, Wisconsin, with an Australian artist named Chris Whitley, whom he had started recording at Royal recording studio a week prior. They had started the sessions in Memphis, but Gaines got the feeling the artist was getting stressed out and suggested that they move to a different location. "I had worked at the studio once before," Gaines says. "It was attached to the hotel that had once been part of the old Playboy club. It was a beautiful setting and the hotel was rarely busy."

Gaines was working with the artists on vocals and miscellaneous overdubs. He knew that Stevie Ray Vaughan was playing that weekend with Eric Clapton and several other acts at Alpine Valley, a fairly short drive away.

"I had talked to Chris Layton about coming to see the show on the second night they were there, since we would be working the first night. The morning of the show, I got a call from Kevin Chisholm, Santana's manager, asking if I could come down to the World Theater and mix a live radio show for them. I said yes, of course. It was more than a three-hour drive to get there, though, which meant that after doing the show, there was no way I could get back in time to see Stevie.

"Early the next morning, I got a call from Chris, saying they had borrowed one of Eric Clapton's helicopters to get back to Chicago, but Stevie never made it; they were missing, he said. Later that morning he called again and said they had found their bodies. Everyone had died when the helicopter crashed. I couldn't believe it. I was supposed to be at that show. The next couple of days were pretty difficult, after getting that news.

"Later I was talking to Stevie's guitar tech about that night, and he had some interesting things to say about what occurred before, during, and after the show. He said that Stevie felt something was special about that night, although they had no idea what the future had in store."

CHAPTER 31

Minding Time in Memphis

1989

THOUGH HE DIDN'T REALIZE IT at the time he was working with Stevie Ray Vaughan and Double Trouble, Gaines was about to return to his roots. He was working in Memphis with the group when he received a call from his housekeeper in San Francisco. She told him that a woman had knocked on the door and asked whether he would be interested in selling his house. She had even made an offer with a price she was willing to pay.

At the time, Gaines's father, who also lived in Memphis, had been ill for some time. Moving back to Memphis to be close to his father seemed like a good idea to Gaines. He asked his housekeeper to get the woman's information for follow-up.

Gaines had been traveling out of town quite frequently. Fortunately, though, he had a neighbor in San Francisco who was a realtor. He contacted her and explained the situation, requesting that she ask the woman to give him three or four days to look for a house in Memphis.

"In the mornings, before the sessions, I would look at houses. I found one I liked and asked my realtor to put the deal together. After selling my house, and while we were in LA doing the mix, I had movers come in and pack, and then I went home for two days and moved. It happened that fast."

Around the same time, Gaines's attorney advised Gaines to meet with Jimi Jamison, the lead singer of Survivor, about doing a record. Survivor is most well known for the song "Eye of the Tiger," which was also the theme for the 1982 movie *Rocky III*, starring Sylvester Stallone. Jamison, who had joined the group in 1984, lived in Memphis, and after he and Gaines met, Jamison asked Gaines whether he could start the sessions once he was moved back to Memphis. Gaines agreed, and the deal was made.

At the same time, Gary Belz, owner of Kiva Studios in Memphis, had learned that Gaines was moving back, and he asked Gaines whether he would base himself out of Kiva and help him manage the studio. Gaines reports that all of this transpired in the space of about four days.

"After a couple of weeks of settling in, we started Jimi Jamison's record," Gaines relates. "We didn't work every day, because he was also doing some gigs. Jimi was a great rock singer as well as one of the nicest guys I've ever met.

"We had a guitarist/arranger working with us, and he wanted to try out some new computer programs for triggering and making up parts. This was all pretty new to me, but I said I was willing. We were using Jimi's local band, and they didn't have a lot of recording experience. For them to have someone like me analyzing everything they played was a new experience. The songs took more of a pop-rock feel as opposed to the strict rock approach that Jimi had previously been known for. Unfortunately, I don't think that worked in our favor."

Nevertheless, the project was moving at a pretty good pace when, about halfway through the recording process, Jamison got a call from Sylvester Stallone. "He wanted us to record a song for his new movie, *Lockup.* I talked to him and asked what he was looking for and when he needed it. I recall that while we were talking, he was mostly speaking from the phone in his limo, and to me, he sounded just like his character Rocky. He said he needed the song right away, which is typical for movie people. They always need it right away."

As a result, Gaines and Jamison immediately stopped what they were doing and brought in the band to record the track for the movie. "I informed the studio that we were going to be working sixteen to twenty hours a day in order to get the song to Stallone on time. I basically had the studio lock us in, and then we got going." Gaines and the artists finished the song in three days. Gaines drove it to the airport at midnight and arranged for it to be hand-delivered to Stallone. "Stallone loved it," Gaines says. "He was very close to Jimi's record label, and they loved it as well."

Around this time, Gaines had noticed that a few business details at Kiva Studios weren't going the way he expected. "Don't get me wrong; I love Gary Belz, but at the same time, we didn't agree on some things. There were some extra charges billed to my session a couple of times, and that didn't sit well with me. As we were getting close to wrapping things up, Gary and I had some discussions about those problems. I didn't really want to get into it, but I felt that if I didn't, there were going to be problems later on as well."

Wanting to ensure that he had a back door if one was needed, Gaines decided to call John Fry at Ardent Studios, also located in Memphis. "I asked him about the possibility of working out of his studio. After we talked for a while, he told me to come on over and he would take care of my needs. I ended up taking the last recording that was left to do for Jimi and going to Ardent. I felt bad leaving Gary, because he had helped me with the Stevie Ray sessions. However, Ardent had some great engineers working for the studio. One of them was John Hampton, who became one of my go-to guys."

In fact, both Hampton and Fry were cornerstones of the music industry in Memphis, and it was a double shock when both men died within a week of each other in 2014.

Jim Gaines would end up working steadily out of Ardent for six or seven years, and he still does, on occasion. "The management and crew there became like family to me," he says now. "But I still miss John Fry and John Hampton. May they rest in peace."

CHAPTER 32

Seeing the Sights in Europe

1990

ABOUT THIS TIME, GAINES received an unexpected call from an American agent who wanted to know whether he would be interested in working with a French guitarist named Louis Bertignac who was forming a new group, to be known as Les Visiteurs. Previously Bertignac was in a group called Téléphone, serving as lead singer and guitarist.

After doing a little research on the artist and the proposed project, Gaines agreed to do it. The idea was to bring the band to Memphis to cut tracks and then go to Brussels to do the overdubs before finally venturing to Paris to do the mix.

"There was a bass player named Corine in the band who was about seven months pregnant," Gaines recalls. "I was surprised that they let her fly across the ocean in that advanced state of pregnancy. I'm sure the reason for finishing it over there had a lot to do with her condition."

The tracking was done at Ardent Studios, and according to Gaines it all went pretty well. Two of the musicians didn't speak English, so that presented a problem at times. "I also remember that the drummer's headphones wouldn't stay on," Gaines says. "He would shake his head a lot while he was playing, and they would drop off. We even taped them on his head with duct tape, which meant that he had to walk around with them on his head even when he wasn't working. At the end of the day we had to cut them off, meaning that some of his hair came off as well. The weird thing was, I think he loved it. I had certainly never done that before."

When they were finished with the tracking in Memphis, Gaines was scheduled to fly to Brussels via Detroit. He had booked a flight with Northwest Airlines through a travel agent. Later, while watching the news, Gaines was chilled to hear the announcer say that his flight had received a bomb threat. About a year earlier, Pan American flight 103 had been blown up over Lockerbie, Scotland. Gaines immediately called his travel agent and told him to change his flight. "I'm sure that plane was checked out very well before taking off, but I wasn't going to be on it," Gaines insisted.

Upon arriving in Brussels, Gaines found the studio to be first class. The Guinean artist Mory Kanté was there recording as well. Though not well known in the United States, Kanté was very famous in Europe, having had a number 1 hit in Belgium, Finland, the Netherlands, and Spain with a song titled "Yé Ké Yé Ké." Gaines, who greatly admired his work, was delighted to get to meet him.

"Overdubs on the Bertignac project were going a little slow," Gaines explains. "It seems that Louis and Corine, the bass player, had been a couple at one time. So here she was, pregnant with someone else's baby. There was clearly tension between them."

Overall, however, the situation was very pleasant. "We had cooks cooking for us every day, and I've never had so much rabbit in my life. It was served almost constantly. Personally, I would have loved to have seen some beef or chicken."

Gaines remembers that at one point, the band wanted to get some pot, so they drove to Amsterdam to make the purchase. "You could buy pot there in certain bars and various other locations," he explains. "You could even buy it on the street. We went into a bar located next to a police station, and in the back there was a pot area. The band was able to buy marijuana, but I couldn't even get anything to drink except for fruit juice. Even now, I'm not sure how that worked."

While Gaines and the group were in Amsterdam, they went to the famous club Paradiso and saw the group the Sugar Babies, who were very big in Europe at the time. Gaines would later produce a live album with blues guitarist Walter Trout, recorded at the Paradiso. "I really love that place," he says. "I think it's one of the best venues I had ever been in. It reminded me of the Fillmore in San Francisco."

Gaines also developed a taste for Belgian chocolate while he was there. "It was the best chocolate I ever tasted. Needless to say, I brought a lot home. Going downtown in Brussels was also a great treat. The buildings are very old, but they were being used and maintained. It was like being in a living history book."

After finishing the overdubs, Gaines drove to Paris to start mixing. They worked in a studio called the Bunker, which had been an old German command center during the Second World War. The front door was made of sheets of steel that were about a foot thick. The walls themselves were four feet thick. It even had an escape tunnel from the building that came out across the street.

"While I was mixing in Studio A, the composer Vangelis was scoring a movie in Studio B," Gaines says. "I got to meet him and to see and hear his setup. It was amazing." Vangelis, who produced scores for such memorable films as *Chariots of Fire* and *Blade Runner,* is still considered one of the most influential figures in the development of electronic music.

"My Paris hotel was only two blocks from the Eiffel Tower," Gaines continues. "I saw it every morning on my walk. I also got to see Notre Dame, but I came away disappointed. There was graffiti painted on the walls, and homeless people were everywhere. It didn't look like it had been kept up."

While Gaines was in Paris, the Berlin Wall came down. People were going crazy, he recalls. "The French people that I was with at the time didn't want it to come down. They wanted to keep the Germans separated and not have them reunite. They viewed this aspect of history in a decidedly different way than most of the people I knew.

"A short time later I had the opportunity to work in East Germany and actually see what the old wall looked like. I stayed in a hotel that used to be one of the KGB headquarters. We recorded a live album for Joanna Connor and Ruf Records at the famous Frannz Club in what had been known as East Berlin. We had a remote truck that had been brought in from Sweden.

"When Russia pulled out of East Germany, a lot of their soldiers were left there. These guys were on the street, selling the military gear they had taken. It certainly was an interesting time to be there."

On Gaines's last night in Berlin, the record company reps took him and the artists to dinner, where they ordered a $500 bottle of wine. "When the wine steward brought it out, he had a big crew with him," Gaines says, "and everyone in the restaurant stopped to watch. I saved the label from the bottle for a while. I certainly had never witnessed anything like that before."

After this European sojourn, it was time for Gaines to turn his attention from the end of the Cold War and expensive bottles of wine. It was time to head back home to embrace an international experience of a different sort.

A Great Dane

1991

NOT LONG AFTER GAINES'S RETURN from Europe, John Wooler, who worked with Virgin Records, called and asked whether he would take on a project that had been recorded in Los Angeles with the involvement of Michael Jackson's engineer. They had recorded an entire album, Wooler told Gaines, but weren't happy with the results. The artist was a Danish woman named Sanne Salomonsen, who, Wooler indicated, was somewhat similar in style to Madonna. Both artists recorded for Virgin Records.

Wooler told Gaines that they wanted him to record four or five songs that could replace some of the tracks that had been laid down in LA. "I met with Sanne, the head of her Danish record label, and John, and we began discussing exactly what they were looking for," Gaines recalls. "I told them I had only twelve days before I was due to start working on a Blues Traveler record in New York."

Because Ardent was booked, Gaines began looking around for other studios where they could record. He ended up using the Sam Phillips studio. "We used someone's side porch for our rehearsal space," Gaines remembers. "A motorcycle was parked there, and there were grease stains in several places. I found the setup rather embarrassing."

At the time, Phillips's studio wasn't being used all that much for outside sessions like the ones Gaines had planned. It was being used mostly for their own in-house projects. "When I walked in the studio, it reeked of cigarette smoke," Gaines recalls. "I was also putting together musicians that I didn't know anything about and hadn't worked with before. After all, I had only been back in Memphis a short time, so I was relying on recommendations from others. The first day there, I brought in some flowers to put in the vocal booth to offset the smell. That seemed to help."

As the band was arriving, Dave Smith, the bass player, told Gaines that he wasn't sure he could play. He said his shoulder was locked up, and as a result he could barely move his arm. Gaines instructed him to go see a doctor to determine what could be done.

"In the meantime, I had hired two guitar players. So I had one of them play Dave's bass parts to at least get us through the first day. Once we finally got to work, though, we ended up with a track that sounded just like a hit. It was only the second song we cut. The label and the artist were so impressed that they pulled me aside at the end of the day and asked if I could do a whole album instead of a few cuts."

Gaines reminded them that he had only a few days before he was due to be in New York. "They said that most of the budget had been spent in LA, but that they hoped to give me enough to finish up an album."

Gaines and company ended up tracking eight or nine songs. They then moved to Ardent Studios to do overdubs and the mix.

"Again, I was using musicians that I had never worked with or even met," Gaines says. "Some worked out and some didn't. I remember one guitarist who had a reputation as a great player. He walked into the studio with one of those big 7-Eleven cups filled with Scotch and said to me, 'Hey, Gaines, I'm glad to be here, and I'm so high that I could go duck hunting with a rake.'

"That may sound funny, but it's not a good way to start a session. I eventually sent him home, even though I would later use him on other projects. I needed to let him know what I wouldn't put up with. I used Rufus Thomas's son Marvell, and Michael Toles, one of Isaac Hayes's guitar players, along with drummer Steve Potts, with Al Green and Dave Smith on bass, once his shoulder recovered. It was a great rhythm section."

They were working long hours trying to get the sessions finished, Gaines remembers. "Fortunately, Sanne was a great singer, so the vocal tracking went quickly. The musicians and background singers did great, also. The overdubs went well, and when it came time to mix, I brought in a young mixer from Nashville, who had come highly recommended as a rock guy."

They ended up mixing in shifts, with Gaines working eight hours and the recruit from Nashville going in and mixing for eight hours. "I had never mixed like that before, but I had no choice," Gaines insists. "We finished the last day at dawn. I caught a plane four hours later to fly to New York to start rehearsing with Blues Traveler."

The Salomonsen album would be called *Where Blue Begins*, and it became a big hit overseas, going to number 1 and staying there for many weeks. In fact, the album eventually went three times platinum in sales, winning several Danish Grammys.

"It was especially cool because we sold more over there than Janet Jackson and Madonna. Sanne loved it. And so did I," Gaines says.

CHAPTER 34

Bonding with Blues Traveler, Grooving with Gales

1991

GAINES HEADED TO NEW YORK to rehearse with Blues Traveler, but the long hours he had spent finalizing the Salomonsen album took a toll. "I almost fell asleep in the rehearsal room because I had almost no sleep during the last few days," Gaines admits. "I had previously flown out to Steamboat Springs, Colorado, to meet with the band. They were scheduled to play at one venue, but the show had sold out and they needed a bigger place to perform. So they ended up playing the big room at the hotel where I was staying. This band had the same type of fanatical following as the Grateful Dead. Their fans would follow them from show to show, and the same fans would show up at all the different venues."

Gaines remembers Blues Traveler as a great band with top-notch musicians, including John Popper on harmonica, Brendan Hill on drums, Bobby Sheehan on bass, and Chan Kinchla on guitar. They were managed by David Graham, the son of the famous concert promoter Bill Graham. Many of them had started playing together while they were still in school. At that time, most of them lived together in an old convent in Queens. "The studio that we tracked in was also in Queens," Gaines remembers. "It was a huge building, and a lot of film people were using it as well.

"The band requested that I use a couple of their sound guys to help record the album. They had been involved in recording demos earlier, so I had no problem with that idea. The studio was usable, but the odd thing was that they had speakers pointed over our heads. That was unusual. Still, because the group was a jam-style band, getting tracks sounding supertight was not a priority."

John Popper was the leader and wrote most of the songs. Gaines says his harp playing leaned a little more toward jazz than it did rock. "They liked to work at night," he reflects. "So the sessions would end at two or three in the morning."

After tracking, the crew moved to Manhattan to finish overdubs and the mix. "As we were finishing vocals, we had a couple of guest artists doing vocals as well," Gaines continues. "Chris Barron from Spin Doctors did some background parts.

"Gregg Allman also took part. The night he came in, I wasn't sure how the session would go. He had been in LA, working on a movie where he played a club owner who, ironically, was named Gaines. He had supposedly gone through rehab before arriving for our session, but he came walking into the studio with a big drink in his hand. I was wondering how it would go down. Fortunately, he was in good spirits, and we had a pleasant visit for a while. He had worked next to me at Ardent while doing one of the Allman Brothers records, with Tom Dowd producing."

Gaines notes that despite his concerns, Allman was prepared, and he had thoroughly practiced the song. "He was one of two people who perspired more than anyone I've ever known. The other was Otis Redding. While Gregg was singing, he would sweat like crazy. He would stop after a couple of takes and ask for a break to get his breath back. He did a great job for us."

After they finished the session, Gaines thanked Allman and asked whether there was anything he could do for him. "He said, 'Well, Jim, I'm going to be sitting in with someone tomorrow night, and the club doesn't have a B3 organ, so would you rent one for me?' I said that of course I would. So I rented a Hammond B3 for him to play the next night, and he was grateful."

After finishing the vocals, Gaines and company started mixing. They used one of New York's top engineers, Joe Blaney. "Mixing went a little slower than normal, but it came out really well. The album, *Travelers and Thieves*, eventually ended up attaining gold status. The band had another very successful record about two CDs later," Gaines remembers. "I loved working with those guys."

000

While Gaines was recording Blues Traveler, he got a call from Ardent Studios telling him that guitarist Eric Gales and his band would be coming to

New York to do a showcase for an album Gaines had worked on earlier with the Memphis artist and his group.

"I don't think the band had ever been out of Memphis, much less to the big city," Gaines says. "Their management hadn't given them anyone to help take care of them at the time. I told the record company to put them in my hotel so that I could take care of them as much as I could while they were there. They were grateful. At this point in time, I was like their Uncle Jim. I was one of the few people in the business they trusted."

When Gaines had recorded the album a few months earlier, Gales was signed to Ardent's production company as well as to Elektra Records. "He was only sixteen years old when we started the project and was being viewed as the next Jimi Hendrix," Gaines says.

Paul Ebersold, a young engineer at Ardent, had been working with the group to do demos and help them get signed to Ardent. The label, in turn, needed someone with experience to oversee the album.

"I remember that the first time we were in rehearsals, neither Eric Gales nor Eugene, his brother who was also the bass player and singer, even owned a tuner for tuning their instruments. So I went out and bought them both tuners. They both played left-handed, upside-down instruments," Gaines remarks. "But I don't think they actually were left-handed. They loved the idea of working with me because of my work with Stevie Ray Vaughan. Their drummer was Hubert Crawford Jr."

Eugene Gale wrote most of the songs on the album, sharing credit for some with Paul Ebersold, and he also did the vocals on the initial album, *The Eric Gales Band.* Later, the record company wanted Eric to do some vocals on the album *Picture of a Thousand Faces*, but his voice wasn't as strong as Eugene's, so he did only the softer songs.

"I had to wait until Eric got out of high school each day to start the session and I also made sure he got finished in time to do homework at night," Gaines recalls. "Once, while we were doing guitar solos, the lights were down and Eric was in the studio playing. We got a couple of takes, and then he came into the control room, laughing his head off. He told me that he had lost his headphones in the middle of the take and he was able to keep time with the track by watching me nodding my head in time in the control room. That's how we got the take. It was only a three-piece band, but they had a powerful sound."

Once they finished the album, *The Eric Gales Band*, they had to wait until Eric finished school to be able to go out and tour. "Radio loved this record,"

Gaines recalls. "*Guitar Player* magazine called him their Best New Talent. A couple of the songs received lots of airplay. Carlos Santana also loved these guys and really tried to help Eric get to the next level. I ended up doing two records with them, and later I would work with them one more time."

The Galeses had another brother who had played on Beale Street in Memphis. He was referred to as "Little Jimmy King," but his real name was Manuel. "They were signed to the House of Blues label," Gaines explains. "The label called me after the project was supposedly finished and asked if I would go into the studio and do two songs with them, because they weren't happy with the album that had been turned in. So I went into the studio with all three Gales brothers. Eric had gotten involved with some chemical substances by this time. His playing was okay, but when it came time to do his solos, he asked if he could do them without me being present. Naturally, I thought this was strange, but Eugene told me that Eric wouldn't do solos while I was watching.

"'Jim,' Eugene told me, 'he's embarrassed because he knows how you feel about having drugs present during your sessions.' So I told them that I would let them do the solo parts just with Eugene. Eric's life took a downward spiral after this, but thankfully, he has finally got himself back together, and now he's doing well. He's a great player, but he never got the real fame we thought he would achieve."

Collaborating with Collins

1992

ALBERT COLLINS, HOWEVER, was an artist who had achieved plenty, and working with him constitutes one of Jim Gaines's favorite memories. Gaines had gotten a call from John Wooler, who had previously contacted him about working with Sanne Salomonsen, asking whether he would be interested in taking on a new project for Albert Collins, the Texas-born blues guitarist sometimes referred to as "The Iceman." Collins had a large following in Europe, and Wooler indicated to Gaines that they had started the album at a studio in the English countryside. Although they had been working there for a couple of weeks, Collins reportedly wasn't happy with the results they were getting or the place they were working.

Gaines suggested to Wooler that they relocate to Memphis. "I ended up using a studio on Beale Street that hadn't been open very long," Gaines recalls. "They had the size studio I needed as well as the isolation booths I was looking for. We used some of the musicians from Albert's band and some local players as well."

After the players were assembled, they went into rehearsals and started recording. Gaines says Albert was happy being in Memphis and working on Beale Street. "Albert was a great player, and he only played lead guitar," Gaines continued. "Coco Montoya had been playing rhythm guitar with him for a short time. Before that, he had played drums in the band. I also hired Teenie Hodges on guitar as well as his brother Charlie on Hammond organ."

The album would be called *Iceman.* "I remember Teenie, who was not in the best of health, walking in with an oxygen tank and an amp the size of a briefcase," Gaines says. "I told him, 'You're not going to get much of a sound out of those small amps, but you've got to go with what you've got.'"

Gaines recalls that the tracking went well, and he knew that Collins would ensure that they got some great solos while cutting tracks. "The band itself was really strong, and they did a great job," Gaines says.

Before the sessions started, Gaines had discovered a discount western boot store in the area. "Being a Texas boy, Albert loved boots," Gaines remembers. "I told him all about the store, and he wanted to go check it out. I took about three or four of the guys to the store. Everyone—me, my engineer, and Albert—ended up buying boots, all of them made from the same kind of snakeskin. There we were, walking around, all posing with the same boots. The guys even convinced me to buy two more pair while we were there."

The recording went well and everything was finished on time. "Albert and I became good friends," Gaines says. "Our bond was strengthened by our mutual connection to Stevie Ray Vaughan, who had always looked up to Albert and gained inspiration from his work. I also learned that Albert had performed with George Thorogood ["Bad to the Bone"] at one time."

The album *Iceman* hit the rock charts in England, and the label was very satisfied with the success it attained both in Europe and the United States. The next album Gaines recorded for Collins was called *Collins Mix.* "That album was one of those projects where the record label was wanting to release older songs but couldn't because the material had previously been released by another label. The solution was to redo some of the older songs again and call it a 'best of' album. As a result, we ended up recording some of Albert's older material with a new band and newer arrangements. In addition, I was starting to record another project for Albert at the same time that featured some new songs.

"I picked a smaller studio to rehearse, and from there I had plans to move to a larger studio for the actual tracking. The studio was called Cotton Row. But rehearsals went so well that I thought, 'Heck, let's start recording right here.' I asked the owner if we could stay and go into tracking mode, and he agreed. Albert was comfortable there. I had him set up to play from the control room with me, and he loved it. He had never done that before."

Before the Cotton Row sessions started, Collins had gone over to Ardent Studios to play on a B. B. King record he was recording, *The Summit.* In return, King came over to Cotton Row and contributed to Collins's album.

"When King arrived, he asked me what I wanted him to play," Gaines says.

"I suggested he add some classic B. B. licks, and he did. He was such a nice person. When we finished, I asked him and Albert to tell some stories about how they went about collecting money for their gigs back in the old days. I sure wish I had recorded those tales they told me. One of them would tell a great story, and then the other would share one of his. We were dying from laughter. What a treat that was!"

Gaines remembers that on one occasion while he was recording with Collins, he went to pick up two of the musicians at the hotel where the group was staying. "As I came around the corner, I saw Albert's bus parked out front. There was a huge black cloud of smoke coming out of the back. I looked up and there was Albert walking out of the cloud, like a scene from a movie. He was actually trying to repair the bus.

"I also remember that once while we were tracking, my engineer turned to me and said, 'Jim, look at the drummer. When he turns his head, his hair doesn't move.' I looked at him, and sure enough, when his head turned, his hair was still pointed forward. It was very strange. He was wearing a toupee, and it was one funny sight. We had to duck under the console because we were laughing so hard."

Gaines, Collins, and the musicians didn't get enough new material recorded for an additional album, so they decided to wait for another time. "Later when I was working with Carlos Santana in Sausalito, Albert was performing at a Bay Area club called Slim's. One of the guys on the crew was always taking photos, so he took some shots of Albert while he was playing live there. Carlos had this great shot of Albert playing and, later, for my birthday, he had it framed for me. That was the start of what became my 'Albert wall.'"

Gaines would reconnect with Collins later, but not on such happy terms. "His manager called me one night and told me if I wanted to talk to him, now would be a good time," Gaines remembers. "I didn't realize Albert was that sick. I got on the phone with him and asked how he was doing. He said, 'Jim, I don't feel well.' I told him, 'Man, you gotta get better and get well so we can finish our record and go to the boot store.' He laughed. Then I mentioned that he had never signed a CD for me, and I asked him if he could do that. He said he would. Sadly, he passed away soon after our conversation. Later, I got this beautiful letter from J. B., saying how much I had lifted Albert's spirits that night. He also had a signed CD for me. I was very touched. I took the letter and had it framed with the CD, just like I would do with a gold record. And that completed my Albert Collins wall. I'll always miss him."

CHAPTER 36

El Tri, Triumphant

1995–1997

THE MEXICAN DIVISION of Warner Bros. Records called and asked Gaines whether he would be interested in working with a blues-rock band called El Tri. Gaines describes them as "a Mexican bad-boy band": think Guns N' Roses, Aerosmith, or even the Rolling Stones. Led by Alex Lora and his wife, Chela, the band definitely knew how to rock. In fact, there were times when their lyrics couldn't be played on the radio, Gaines says, because they had a habit of criticizing the government in some very colorful language.

Gaines recalls flying down to Mexico City to meet the group and then going out to lunch. "During the meal, one of the waiters recognized them," he remembers. "Before we had a chance to leave, there was a near riot caused by people wanting to ask them for autographs or simply say hello. That's how popular they were."

The two leaders of the band, Alex and Chela Lora, spoke English, but several members of the band didn't. However, Gaines explains that Alex Lora sang in Spanish, which was a challenge when it came to doing vocals because Gaines didn't know exactly what the lyrics were. Going in, he knew only a small amount of Spanish, but the Loras had him speaking a lot of it before the project was finished.

In fact, Gaines ended up recording three albums for the prolific group: their twenty-eighth, twenty-ninth, and thirty-first records. He says Alex Lora had initially been signed when he was about fifteen years old.

"We recorded the first album at the Indigo Ranch studio," Gaines explains. "The studio was on top of a mountain in Malibu. The studio is said to be haunted, perhaps because it was built on what had been an Indian burial site. The owner, Richard Kaplan, relates that he once had some Native American spiritual leaders come out and do a couple of ceremonies to please the spirits."

The studio was also a hangout for a lot of old movie stars like John Barrymore and his crowd. It was also owned at one time by the Stetson family, of hat fame, who used the property as a getaway from Hollywood.

"To get to the studio, one had to take a very narrow winding drive up into the mountains," Gaines says. Because of the lack of easy access, the studio provided housing for clients. But once you were up there, Gaines says, the view of the ocean was incredible.

"Alex brought some of his cooks up from Mexico to prepare meals for us, and we had some great dining as a result," Gaines remembers. "I ended up staying at the famous Malibu Beach Inn in a room that hung out over the water. If you went to the grocery store in Malibu, you'd see lots of actors there as well."

The name of the album they were working on was *Cuando tú no estás* (When you are not here). "One of the songs was called 'Virgen morena,'" Gaines continued. "It's about the Virgin Mary, and the title means something like 'Brown-Haired Virgin.' Alex asked me if I could possibly get Carlos Santana to play a solo on it. I contacted Carlos, and he agreed to do it. Later I would fly to San Francisco and record his track. He loved the song. It was a very special tune, and the band had never really approached one like it. It also got lots of airplay.

"At the record release show, thousands of people showed up. It also was nominated for a Latin Grammy. The next two records would also be nominated, but we never won. Working with El Tri was lots of fun. There would be times they were telling jokes in Spanish and I would be laughing along with them, not because I knew what they were saying but just because they were having so much fun."

The follow-up album they did was called *Fin de Siglo*. "We recorded most of it at Capitol Studios," Gaines says. "When we were done tracking, we wanted to bring in a guest singer from Spain for one of the tracks. The singer we had in mind was the famous singer-songwriter and producer Andrés Calamaro. To get him, we would have to fly him here or we would have to go to him in Spain. Fortunately, Capitol had just gotten these special phone lines put in that would allow us to play back our track to a Spanish studio. That way, Andrés could sing in the studio over there while we recorded him in our studio. This technique had been used a couple of times in the past, so fortunately, the technology had been worked out beforehand. I think Stevie Wonder was the first one to use it. However, I took the precaution of sending a tape to Spain for him to record on in case something went wrong. So here we were, back in LA, recording a vocal from Spain. Even when we were speaking with Andrés on our talk-back, it was just like he was in our room. Alex has always been someone who tries to stay up with technology, as well as a terrific bass player."

The final album Gaines did with El Tri was titled *No podemos volar* (We can't fly). "We recorded this album at West Lake Studios," Gaines says. "The room we used was the one they had built for Stevie Wonder, and it was a great studio. I had been there once before to visit one of Stevie's sessions with a friend who had recorded with him when he was in Detroit, with Motown. I only got to say a quick hello, because Stevie was on the phone at the time. But I got to see his setup. I had worked with him one night in San Francisco.

"The record with El Tri went smoothly and was recorded fairly quickly. This album was also nominated for a Latin Grammy, the same year as Santana's *Supernatural* record, which I helped mix. I had three records nominated that year!" (In addition to *Supernatural* and *No podemos volar*, the third album was *Live in Chicago*, by Luther Allison; more of that story is in the next chapter.)

"Alex and Chela Lora are two wonderful people," Gaines says in summation. "It was a pleasure working with them." And his next venture would be equally satisfying.

CHAPTER 37

The Late and Great Luther Allison

1994–1997

GAINES WAS ORIGINALLY INTRODUCED to blues great Luther Allison by Thomas Ruf, the founder and namesake of Ruf Records. Gaines was familiar with the label because he had already recorded a few projects for the company.

"Luther was a blues and soul singer who was originally from Arkansas, just like me," Gaines explains. "We grew up about thirty miles from each other. Luther had originally recorded for another label several years prior to our meeting. He had been based in Paris but had very few bookings in the US." Gaines relates that Allison was quite popular with Parisian audiences and had even opened several times for the famous French singer Johnny Hallyday.

"He had a few albums that were released in Europe," Gaines continues. "He and Thomas wanted me to do a record with him that might bring him some renewed success in the American market."

Allison wanted to bring his French band to the States for the recording, but Gaines had always been hesitant to use an artist's backing band because he found there was a big difference between the quality of their musicianship onstage and in the studio. "I had no idea how good these guys were, but I agreed to try," Gaines recalls.

"We got them to Memphis, where I had two days of rehearsals scheduled. During the first day, I realized immediately that while they may have been a good live band, it was going to be difficult getting good tracks from them. The only player I felt had potential to be able to do the job was Luther's American guitar player, Jim Solberg.

"During the initial rehearsal, I asked the drummer to take me to the first verse of the song we were playing. He said to me, 'What is a verse?' I knew at that point that we had a problem. So I told Luther that I was going to send his guys out to dinner and bring my guys in to jam with him for a hour or so, so that he could hear the difference in the players. After the first half hour, his eyes went wide and his smile got really big. He told me he now understood what I wanted."

Gaines hired his band for the recording, whereupon Allison asked Gaines whether he would fire the Parisian musicians and send them home. "Luther knew he would have to deal with them when he got back to Paris. Nevertheless, he hid out in his room so he wouldn't have to talk to them."

Gaines reports that he took them all down to the bar, bought them a round of drinks, and told them that he would be sending them home and using his musicians instead. "Naturally, they were devastated. The bass player might have been good enough, but I wanted my entire crew. Meanwhile, they had planned on being in the US for two weeks, and some of them asked if they could hang out and watch for a couple of days. I actually ended up coming up with some small parts for them, just so they could be on the record. I'm sure they hated me, but business always comes first."

Gaines came to discover that Luther Allison had some odd habits. "Luther was a smoker, but he hid it from his then-girlfriend and partner, Rocky Brown," he remembers. (Allison and Brown were subsequently married). "While we were working, he would bring in his smokes and give them to my assistant engineer, who would hold them for him. Then the two of them would sneak out to smoke. It seemed pretty obvious to me what was going on, but maybe Rocky never caught on."

Gaines also recalls that Allison needed reading glasses, but he refused to use them. So when it came to the lyrics, they had to blow them up big enough for him to be able to read them. Two or three music stands were required just to spread the lyrics sheets out for him. He also had to have his shined shoes on at all times. He would bring in his house shoes, which were shined, and wear them instead of his regular ones. Gaines says he took to calling Allison "the shoeshine man."

"When Luther was in his booth singing, he would give one hundred percent every time," Gaines says. "When the band was slacking off a bit, I had to get on them and encourage them to give me a better performance just so they would keep up with him."

Fortunately, the recording went well, and all the session musicians did a great job, according to Gaines. The album was eventually released with two different titles. In Europe it was called *Bad Love*, after one of the songs. Bruce Iglauer of Alligator Records, the company that eventually released the album in the United States, didn't like negative titles on songs or album covers, so the album was titled *Soul Fixin' Man* in the States. Gaines notes that an American record deal hadn't been secured until after the album was completed, when it was signed with Alligator Records.

Gaines and Iglauer had never worked together until that point. "He insisted on having complete control of his projects," Gaines says. "However, when it came to the Luther Allison albums, I had the control, because of my relationship with the artist. It drove Iglauer crazy, because he had no say in what I did or how I did it. Nevertheless, I would end up doing a couple of projects for him later on. He and I bumped heads a few times. However, we eventually became friends—kind of."

Soul Fixin' Man would go on to win several prestigious W. C. Handy Awards (now called Blues Music Awards) from the Blues Foundation. It proved to be Allison's big comeback record and opened up a lot of new venues where he was able to perform.

The second record Gaines recorded with him was called *Blue Streak*. It was released in 1997. "By that time, Luther knew how I worked and what to expect when it came to my recording technique. I tried using some of his American band, as well as my musicians. It worked out fine, with only a couple of changes. I had to send his drummer home due to his negative attitude, but most of the other guys were fine. And of course, Bruce Iglauer had to change some song titles. For example, 'Cherry Red Wine' was a very good song, but it started out having a different title. Nevertheless, it got a lot of airplay and was covered by a few other people. It also brought him a few more W. C. Handy Awards. The record also brought him more festival gigs. He played one with Santana and that made him very happy. Both men really hit it off with each other."

Gaines was working in the studio with the well-known blues guitarist Jimmy Thackery on the night of the Handy Awards when Luther came in with a cardboard box filled with his awards. "He wanted to show them to me," Gaines says. "Jimmy was sitting there watching, and it was obvious he was a little upset because he had never been nominated for an award, much less won. Still, Jimmy and I worked well together and we ended up doing three albums together."

Gaines was delighted by Allison's success. "We became like brothers. The third album we did together was called *Reckless.* I had gotten a song from Jerry Williams several months before we started recording. Jerry had sent me various songs over the years, but this one in particular, 'Living in the House of Blues,' caught my ear. I called Jerry and asked if I could get a hold on it until I could get Luther in the studio to record it. He told me that the people from the *House of Blues* radio show had already put a hold on it, but they weren't using it. When it came time to start recording Luther's new album, I called Jerry back and said I wanted that song right away. Jerry called the other people and told them that I would be using the song. It went on to win Song of the Year in addition to other awards at the next W. C. Handy Awards show."

Another song Gaines recorded for Allison came from an unexpected source. "My wife, Sandy, and I had started dating at the time," Gaines says. "Sandy and James Solberg wrote this song about me and about us as a couple that was called 'Just as I Am.' We played it for Luther, and he immediately decided that he wanted it. He added a few lines and subsequently recorded it. He also did a version in Paris as a duet, which was released only in Europe." Later, when Sandy and Gaines were married in Las Vegas, they arranged to have that song played for their march down the aisle, but Allison would not live to see that day.

"I had submitted several songs to Luther during our time together, and he always recorded at least one of them. One of the final things I did with him turned into a very special project. It was one of those albums that had different artists recording cover songs that paid tribute to a particular artist. This one was an album of Rolling Stones songs called *Paint It Blue.* Luther was asked to do one song, so while he was on the road, I talked to him about which one he wanted to do. During his concerts, he would do a medley of different songs that included one Stones song in particular, 'You Can't Always Get What You Want.' He played it for me over the phone. I took the idea and cut a track, putting horns and background vocals on it. That way, all he had to do was walk in and sing and play a little.

"However, when he came in that day to record, he didn't look very good. I asked him what was wrong. He said, 'Jim, I almost walked off the stage the other night, and I keep running into my mic stand during the show.'"

Gaines immediately called the record company and told them to take Allison off the road because he wasn't well. A few weeks later, Allison was in Madison, Wisconsin, where he and Rocky had a cabin. While there, he was involved in a small automobile accident. He went to the hospital and found out that he had both lung and brain cancer, both of which had progressed significantly. He lasted only a few weeks after that, dying on August 12, 1997, five days after his fifty-eighth birthday.

"When I got the call, "Gaines says, "I felt like someone had punched me in the stomach. I couldn't breathe. I hid out in my house for three days. I didn't want to talk to anyone or see anyone."

Reckless won another three W. C. Handy Awards, including Song of the Year, for "Living in the House of the Blues." "The final thing I did for Luther was to finish and mix an unreleased live album that had mostly been recorded at the Chicago Blues Festival," Gaines says. That record, mentioned in the last chapter, received a Grammy nomination.

"Rest in peace, my brother. I still miss you."

Later Gaines would work with Luther Allison's son, Bernard. "Luther had taught him to be a real blues man. He had cowritten some songs with his dad and had played with him in Paris. Bernard and I recorded several projects together, and we're planning on doing another one soon. He's a great kid."

CHAPTER 38

Soaring with Santana

1989–1999

AFTER GAINES MOVED BACK to Memphis in 1989, he would continue working with Carlos Santana off and on for the next ten years. During the fall of 1989, he went back to the Bay Area and the Plant to work on Santana's *Spirits Dancing in the Flesh* album. This also happened to be the year of the big California earthquake.

"I remember that the hotel I was staying at, the Corte Madera, was a two-story wooden building," Gaines relates. "I had stayed there many times over the years. A night or two before the big one, I remember waking up in the middle of the night, feeling the building shudder. I had been through several earthquakes and I knew how it felt, and this felt like it was definitely an earthquake.

"The afternoon of the quake, we were working on organ overdubs with Chester Thompson, and Carlos was there. Carlos and one of the office people decided to go to the shopping mall while Chester and I finished up our parts. I had Chester's Hammond organ in the control room with me, and the Leslie speaker was out in the studio. There was a lot of low end being generated by the B3 for the part we were doing, and we had the speakers up pretty loud. It was then that I felt something strong in the room that didn't seem normal. Chester looked at me and I turned to look at him, and we both said at the same time, 'What are you doing?' Suddenly, we knew we both had to get out of there."

They headed for the door. "There was an outside door within a few feet that went out to the alleyway. Unfortunately, it was locked. So we headed through the building towards the front, with other people joining us as we headed towards the parking lot. Everyone seemed to pretty much know what we were in for."

Once they got outside, Gaines says, the ground felt like it was rolling under their feet. "It felt almost like stepping on a waterbed for a moment. We were all standing around waiting for the aftershocks. I got in my rental car and turned on the radio for us to hear about what was happening. The announcers were going crazy, insisting that this was 'The Big One.'"

While all this was happening, the World Series was taking place at Candlestick Park. "As we were listening, the announcer said that part of the Bay Bridge had collapsed, and part of the elevated freeway in Oakland had fallen onto itself. I knew that wasn't going to be good. There was normally a packed highway over there, but fortunately, with the ball game taking place, the highway wasn't packed. Unfortunately, though, several people were crushed by the top part that had collapsed."

Gaines would later learn that one of the Santana crew members was on the Golden Gate Bridge at the time of the quake. "He said it was all he could do to hold his car in the lane to keep it from going head-on into someone coming from the opposite direction. I've been on that bridge many times in fog and wind, and I can attest to the fact that it's almost impossible to stay in your lane even during a normal time, because the bridge always seems to sway."

Gaines remembers that the phone lines at the studio were also knocked out, except for the fax line. This was well before cell phones were everywhere, so it was difficult for them to call anyone.

"After the aftershocks had settled down, we decided to try to get home. My hotel was only about four miles away, but the freeway was packed with people leaving the city. It took me at least two hours to get there. The studio had some damaged equipment, but we managed to get it up and going in a day or two. One of the studios I used, which was down the street, had its main board twisted. I still remember that day as if it happened yesterday. I have copies of the newspaper from the next two days, each with big bold headlines, all about the quake."

000

All this was taking place in the middle of recording Santana's *Spirits Dancing in the Flesh* album. Several guest artists participated in the project, including Bobby Womack, Peter Wolf, Wayne Shorter, Vernon Reid, and the Edwin Hawkins Singers. In addition, singer Alex Ligertwood was back with the band.

"Making this album was a little scattered, and it was done in different parts with the different artists involved," Gaines remembers. "Vernon Reid was coming off the success he had attained with his band Living Colour. He was terrific, and very creative as well." *Rolling Stone* listed Reid at number 66 on its roster of "100 Greatest Guitarists of All Time."

"Bobby Womack [who had been a backing guitarist for the great Sam Cooke] was great when doing his parts. Naturally, Wayne Shorter [saxophonist for Herbie Hancock, Weather Report, and others] was always great to work with. We did one song that had him playing sax in the control room. It was ostensibly just for a reference track, but when the take was over, he suggested that we keep it.

"When we were starting the song, Wayne brought out these different charts. He spread them out over the entire console. Carlos looked at me with panic on his face. It's not that he couldn't read music, but he had never seen anything like this that he had to play to before. That caused Wayne to start laughing at Carlos and Chester Thompson. Ultimately, quite a few people worked on this project, and we had a lot of fun working with all of them."

In 1991, Gaines recorded Santana's next project, which was called *Milagro*. It was destined for Polydor, Santana's new record label. Guests on the album included Carlos's brother Jorge Santana, vocalist Tony Lindsay, percussionist Walfredo Reyes, singer Linda Tillery, and others, including Bill Graham's recitation of an intro piece dedicated to Miles Davis and John Coltrane. The album took several months to record and didn't get the response the label had been expecting. "I'm not sure Polydor promoted it as well as CBS had done with the previous albums," Gaines observes.

Gaines's next project with Santana was called *Sacred Fire,* a live album recorded in South America that became the band's second album for Polydor. "We took a lot of gear to South America to record this project," Gaines explains. "We recorded it in several locations, including Mexico City and Venezuela, which is where most of the performances took place."

Gaines recalls several interesting things that happened while they were there. "When we got to Mexico City, the Miss World pageant was taking place in our hotel. The entire lobby was filled with press people. All these gorgeous contestants were posing for the photographers and doing press interviews. Then, when we got to the concert site to set up our gear—in a soccer locker room—it had just been cleaned with some kind of chemical that smelled so bad we could barely breathe. We had to bring in some huge fans just to get the smell out. I mean, it was bad.

"Then, when we got to Venezuela, we found out that there was a nationwide teacher protest. There was a lot of turmoil in the streets. To make matters worse, the country's president had just been deposed. In our hotel they were hosting the new president's state dinner, so the hotel was full of security people and they all seemed really nervous. I was stopped several times and my shoulder bag was searched repeatedly."

Once they reached the concert site in Venezuela, they discovered that it was fairly small. During sound check, Gaines recalls, there was an argument between the promoter and the owner of the PA system. Apparently the promoter hadn't paid his rental fee, and they were dismantling the speakers in order to take them away.

"Fortunately, it finally got settled. However, in the middle of the show, someone either jumped or fell into the amps that drove the PA, tearing off the main cable that fed the system. As a result, the system went down. Carlos realized what was going on and kicked his monitor speaker forward. It was still working, so it gave the audience something to listen to, at least. Someone finally replaced the cable. But we had no audience microphones picking up the PA."

Ultimately, Gaines observes, the album was simply a way for the new label to rerelease some older material.

000

In 1994, Gaines attended the ill-fated Woodstock Two festival. As most people recall, twenty-five years earlier, the original Woodstock had been a launching pad for Santana's original band. They hadn't been booked for it initially, but because another act dropped out, their manager at the time, Bill Graham, had gotten them on the bill. Of course, they went over really well and their performance helped elevate their national profile.

"While we were driving to Woodstock Two, the people who were leaving looked to us like refugees," Gaines remembers. "It had been raining and fairly cold, and they weren't prepared. The site wouldn't let them bring tent pegs or anything sharp into the site, so they couldn't get their tents up. Out of desperation, they were wrapping themselves in plastic sheets. They looked awful.

"When we got there, the backstage area looked like a small city. I was told that they estimated there were ten thousand people back there. There was also a steady stream of ambulances leaving the place. There was a small lake or river behind the site, and several people had drowned."

Because the grounds had been a pasture at one time, Gaines recalls, the venue was very wet and very muddy. Nevertheless, three or four stages were going constantly. As a result, the spectators were also all wet and muddy. There was a big half circle in the middle of the crowd where water streamed out for "showers," Gaines says. "As we were being brought in, we noticed that there were people tearing down the fences so they could get in for free, and there wasn't enough security to stop them. I was there to record Santana's set. Several years earlier, I had mixed a few tracks from the original Woodstock performance."

The stages were set up in the round, with a wall down the middle of a rotating platform, splitting the stage into two sections. While one band was playing out front, the next act would be setting up on the opposite side. When it was time for the next set to start, they would simply rotate the stage. Gaines says it seemed to be a great idea.

"I was onstage when Green Day was playing. Someone from the audience threw a big mud and grass glob that landed at the band's feet. The singer picked it up and threw it back, which was the wrong thing to do, as it turned out. A lot of people started to throw big clods onstage, and several hit the guys in the group. One of them got a big cut on his head, and the drummer got hit as well. They ended up being pulled off early because clearly they were getting hurt. I felt sorry for them, because they were a great band and just trying to have some fun.

"I wanted to buy a T-shirt, but that meant going out through the mud and the people to get to the vendor. I decided that wasn't going to happen. Fortunately, when I was at the airport leaving town, I ran into a young teenage boy who had one. It even had mud on it. I made him an offer he couldn't refuse, and I still have the T-shirt.

"It was an amazing sight to see one hundred thousand–plus people having fun and listening to some great music, even if it was in the mud and the cold." Fortunately, Gaines would soon find himself in warmer and considerably more comfortable environs.

CHAPTER 39

Santana Grabs Some Grammys

1991–2000

GAINES RECORDED SANTANA'S *Supernatural* album in 1998. Prior to that, Carlos Santana had briefly been signed to Island Records, though he had never recorded an album for that label. Gaines isn't sure why he didn't, but the talk at the time was that he either didn't connect personally with the management or disagreed with the direction they wanted him to go.

"We had gone into the studio at that time to record some songs," Gaines remembers. "I think they were mostly meant as demos to shop around, but I'm not sure. In the meantime, Carlos had meetings with Clive Davis of Arista Records about signing with him. Clive and Carlos had a long relationship, going back to the old CBS days. So, not surprisingly, they agreed to a new deal."

Gaines had his own impression of Davis. "Clive is a 'singles' kinda guy," Gaines says now. "He wants songs that sound good on the radio. He gets really involved with his artists. I had dealt with him on some other projects, and I knew that he liked to pick songs for being recorded. On my meetings with him he would dictate several things he wanted, rather than just turning it over to an A&R person. In this case, I was told that Clive wanted to try and connect Carlos with some up-and-coming young talent to be guest artists for the project. He wanted control of at least half the songs that were selected, and Carlos would be responsible for the other half."

Ultimately, the album took over a year, off and on, to record. "A lot of the songs would be almost completed, then they'd be sent to us so that we could put in parts from Carlos, keyboard player Chester Thompson, and percussionist Karl Perazzo to finish the song. Then it would be sent back to the artist or the producers to complete," Gaines says. "On a couple of occasions, I would do the mix. Some of the songs were even created in the studio. For example, a track called 'Maria Maria' was produced by Wyclef Jean, the great rapper from Haiti. He brought in his crew and a new two-person act called Product G&B, whom he had just signed to his production company. They were two young men who were fresh out of high school.

"Carlos had the title and some ideas for the song, so Wyclef took it from there. It was created that night and finished by us the next day. He took it back to New York and finalized it. 'Maria Maria' was a big hit, especially in the club scene. It sold a million singles, was on the *Billboard* Hot 100 for ten weeks, and won a Grammy for Best Pop Performance by a Duo or Group with Vocals."

Another guest artist for the album was Lauryn Hill, who brought in a new singer, Cee-Lo Green. She had started working on the song "Do You Like the Way," which, like "Maria Maria," was written mostly in the studio. "It was interesting having her there because she was very pregnant," Gaines recalls. "She also had her crew there along with her husband, who was some sort of high priest connected to an island religion she was associated with."

Rob Thomas (Matchbox Twenty) was in the studio working on an album, and he sent over a song called "Smooth." It was mostly finished, so Gaines, Santana, and the other musicians put their parts on it and sent it back. "Smooth" became a huge worldwide hit, winning Grammys for Record of the Year, Song of the Year, and Best Pop Collaboration with Vocals.

Dave Matthews was also in the studio working on a project, and Gaines got two songs from him, including "Love of My Life." Everlast (the stage name for artist Erik Francis Schrody) sent them another great song called "Put Your Lights On," which won a Grammy for Best Rock Performance with a Duo or Group Vocal. The album also included a song titled "Yaleo" with Shakara Mutela, a tune named "El farol" with K. C. Porter, and "The Calling" with Eric Clapton. The internationally acclaimed Mexican rock band Maná also made an appearance.

Ultimately, *Supernatural* reached number 1 in the United States for over ten weeks. It also climbed to number 1 in over eleven countries. It won nine Grammys, was named Album of the Year, and also won Album of the Year at the Latin Grammys. It won three other Latin Grammys as well.

Carlos Santana, the first Hispanic musician to win that many Grammys, tied Michael Jackson's record for the most Grammy Awards won in a single night. One news story referred to the 2000 Grammy Awards as "the coronation of Carlos Santana." There were six singles released from the album; *Supernatural* would go on to sell fifteen million copies in the United States and another ten million copies worldwide. "For every song that was released, we worked on almost the same number that were either released later or never released at all," Gaines muses.

The follow-up album was titled *Shaman.* It too featured an array of guest artists and, like *Supernatural,* also took longer to finish. Among the artists for *Shaman* were Chad Kroeger from Nickelback, who was featured on the song "Why Don't You"; Seal (stage name for British musician Henry Olusegun Adeola Samuel), who contributed to "You Are My Kind"; and Michelle Branch, who sang on "Game of Love," a track that made the top 10 and would go on to win a Grammy. Other guests included Musiq Soulchild (Taalib Johnson), opera superstar Placido Domingo, and Christian metal band POD (Payable on Death). Rob Thomas returned to contribute his talent to a song titled "Nothing at All."

Shaman didn't do as well as *Supernatural.* "It's really hard to come back with a follow-up that finds you doing the same thing you did with your big hit," Gaines insists. "But we had some interesting encounters while touring with the album. We did quite a few live television and radio shows, especially in Europe. We were doing the Nobel Peace Prize awards in Norway when former president Jimmy Carter was receiving an award.

"We had Michelle Branch with us to sing 'Game of Love.' We only did this song on special occasions because Santana didn't have a female singer. So here we were doing the song, and she forgot part of the lyric. The show was live in most of Europe, but it was rebroadcast in the US, so that wasn't good by any means. The next day, we flew to London and immediately went to a studio and had her sing the correct lyrics, and I mixed it so it could go out correctly. However, that wasn't the only problem we had with her. During another show that was beamed live to ten countries, she decided that her mic might not be working right, so she traded for one used by one of the other singers without telling us. The levels were very different between the two. As a result, her vocal suddenly disappeared, because the level of the other singer's mic was down. Meanwhile, he sang into her mic, which was turned up for her, and the levels suddenly went crazy. We couldn't figure out what was going on. It was another disaster for us, and it was all broadcast live.

"But at least I did get to shake Jimmy Carter's hand. I just stuck out my hand as security was bringing him by. I said, 'Congratulations, sir,' and he stopped and said, 'Thank you, young man.' Another time, we were doing a show in a nice hall in Munich, Germany, and we had a remote truck on the street, which was quite a way from the stage. It was supposed to be a live radio broadcast. When the truck showed up, it was way underequipped. The console wasn't big enough, and they had extra gear that didn't work or barely worked at all. By the time showtime arrived, I was still trying to get all our mics working. I never got to the percussion section. When the show started, I was on a walkie-talkie to Kevin Chisolm, Santana's manager, about the problem. He asked what I wanted to do about it. I said that there was only one thing we could do, and that was to cancel. He said that he would only hold the band for three or four minutes and then it was up to me.

"So I turned around to the producers and mobile people and said, 'No show!' and I pulled the faders down and blocked the console. I thought they might try to bypass me. By that time, they hated me anyway. After the show I saw Carlos and he asked me what had happened. I told him the story and he said, 'Jim, no percussion, no Santana, and that's why you are here: to protect us as much as possible.'"

Gaines recalls another strange situation that occurred in Lima, Peru. "About two hours after we arrived at the hotel, I got a call from Kevin Chisholm. He said that he needed me to come to his hotel room immediately. He informed me that he might be arrested, in which case he would need me to take over his managing duties. 'Oh Lord, I can't do that,' I replied. Nevertheless, I went to his room, and there was a general there who was in charge of our security, as well as a colonel, some judges, lawyers, and court people. Kevin told me that they were there to arrest Carlos, but he wasn't going to let that happen, and that they would have to take him instead. It seemed that several years earlier, Carlos was supposed to do a show there and had canceled, and now the promoter wanted his money back. After a couple of hours of negotiations, a settlement was reached. In South America at that time, payoffs settled a lot of things."

Still, to make matters worse, while they were in Lima, Gaines reports, one of the foreign embassies had been taken over by rebels, and tension was running high: tanks were on the streets and soldiers were popping up everywhere. The stadium where the concert was to occur was ringed with troops, and they were brandishing a lot of guns, according to Gaines. "As we were going back to our hotel later on, we were even threatened by a man on the street with a gun who attempted to stop our van. It was a mess. The trip to the airport was like a chase scene out of an action movie. I told Carlos that I would never be going back there. Some years later I had to change planes in Lima, and even that didn't go down real well with me."

More Sizzle with Santana

REVIEWING THE 1990S

FROM THE COUNTLESS HOURS spent recording and touring with Carlos Santana, Jim Gaines has scores of memories: some humorous, some heartbreaking, and many thrilling. And occasionally he was also the bearer of information on Santana's behalf that others didn't exactly want to hear.

For example, one year at the Latin Grammys, the program included a tribute to the famed bandleader Tito Puente. The musical portion of the celebration was augmented by a big orchestra, and Puente's son, Tito Jr., was responsible for all the arrangements. "The band was all wearing tuxes," Gaines notes. "So as we were making ourselves comfortable backstage and chatting, one of the young assistants came flying into the room, came over to us, and said, 'Mr. Santana, I'm here to get your measurements for a white tux that you will be wearing tonight.'

"Carlos looked at her and then looked at me, and then told me to tell her that Santana doesn't wear a white tux. I relayed the information, and she got all flustered and then left. A few minutes later, her boss arrived, looking extremely stressed. He said, 'Mr. Santana, everyone in the band will have white tuxes on.' Again, Carlos looks at me and not at him. 'Tell him, Jim,' he said.

"So again I said, 'Mr. Santana isn't going to wear a white tux.' Carlos didn't even look up at him. He was wearing one of his normal Santana-style T-shirts and a beautiful jacket. And that was what he was wearing when he went onstage—end of story."

○○○

Later, Gaines recalls doing an A&E Network live show in New York with Santana. It was in a small hall with a small audience, and the format allowed the crowd to request songs from the artist. "As we were preparing the sound, a guest walked in, and when I realized who it was, I nearly fell over. It was Les Paul," Gaines says.

"His son was with him and he brought Les over so Les could introduce himself. After saying hello, I said to him, 'I want to thank you for my career.' He was a little taken aback because normally people only want to talk about his guitars. But he was also famous for inventing multiple-track recording. He worked with Ampex to build a tape machine that you could play back and record at the same time, developing it for the records he made for his wife, Mary Ford. I told him that because of that innovation, I was able to get a career. It was wonderful to meet him, and he was very nice."

○○○

"The year *Supernatural* was nominated for all those Grammys," Gaines says, "I was also up for two other awards that night. The National Academy of Recording Arts and Sciences (NARAS) had told me that I had to buy a ticket for my wife, Sandy, to attend the show. I really couldn't believe it. Fortunately, the Santana family found out and ended up taking care of her that night. She hung out with Carlos's sister and office manager, and we all had a great time.

"On the ride back to the hotel, the paparazzi found out which cars we were in, and they did everything in their power to get to Carlos, even to the point of trying to block his car at an intersection and storming after us at the hotel. We had to get extra security just to get him to his room. I can see why a lot of famous people get so upset with them."

○○○

But Gaines's time with Santana wasn't always made up of raving fans, exciting performances, and conversations with backstage crews. There was also tragedy, on at least one occasion.

"We were on tour with Santana and doing a show in Nice, France. Wayne Shorter was also there at a stopover on his own tour. Wayne was expecting his wife and niece to arrive that day, so we joined him. I had met his wife several times and was looking forward to greeting her.

"But the TWA flight that Wayne's wife and niece were on went down outside of New York City. When Wayne got the call, no one was sure if there were any survivors or knew what had caused it to crash. We were very concerned, and not only on Wayne's behalf, because Carlos's family was due to arrive the next day from the States. Naturally, Wayne got on the first flight to New York, but he would learn that, tragically, there were no survivors. We were very nervous about Carlos's family coming over, because the initial theory was that a rocket had taken down the TWA flight."

000

The last album Gaines did with Santana was *All That I Am.* It also featured a number of guest artists, including the Black Eyed Peas, Steven Tyler, and Mary J. Blige. Unfortunately, like *Shaman,* it didn't do as well as *Supernatural.* Nevertheless, Gaines still relishes the twenty years that he worked with Carlos Santana and his crew, and he was still looking forward to new opportunities. Gaines would like to send a special thanks to Carlos Santana and his staff and crew: "Thank you for all the wonderful experiences and beautiful music over the years."

CHAPTER 41

When Things Go Wrong

MORE MEMORIES FROM THE 1990S

DURING HIS DECADES WORKING with hundreds of artists from all across the blues, soul, and rock and roll spectrum, Jim Gaines has had his share of experiences with things not going as planned. A perfect example was an occasion when John Wooler, a record producer who is well regarded for his work with many great blues artists, called Gaines about working on a project in Memphis with a well-known Chicago-based guitar player. For the purposes of this story, Gaines has asked that the guitarist remain nameless.

"On the first day of rehearsal, after a quick meeting in the musician's hotel room and not having much time to hear his songs, we set a time to rehearse in the studio with the band," Gaines says. "He showed up three hours late. When he walked in, he had white powder on his mustache and beard. I knew instantly what he had been doing. The rehearsal went very slowly, and so finally I said, 'Let's try again tomorrow, and you set the time that you are really going to be here.' The next day I went in, but there was no artist. I was going over songs with the band when the studio manager came in and told me that I really needed to take a phone call. The artist's manager was on the phone, telling me that our guitarist was not only in Chicago—not Memphis, where we were recording—but also that he was in jail. This was surprising to learn, to say the least. But apparently, he had left his hotel in Memphis right after I saw him, took the group's van, drove to Chicago to buy more drugs, and was then arrested by an undercover officer. Plus, he was already out on bail from another arrest. I also found out that he had spent five thousand dollars of the recording budget on drugs as he left town.

"So here I was with the band, and they have no way of getting home with their gear, since the artist had taken off in their van. I called the record company and told them what was going on. Then I got the band and their gear down to the bus station, bought them tickets home, gave each musician a few dollars for food, and sent them off to Chicago.

"My next phone call was to tell the label I never wanted to hear about this guy again. But six months later I got a letter from the Better Business Bureau, telling me they had a complaint against me. It seems the artist said I had ruined his career because I wouldn't do his record. I just gave the letter to my attorney and said, 'Take care of this.'"

Indeed, when things go wrong, they can go wrong in a very big way. That's reason enough to get the blues. But, as Jim Gaines can also tell you, "getting the blues" doesn't have to be a bad thing.

CHAPTER 42

Here Come the Blues— the Best of the Rest

1989–PRESENT

INDEED, BLUES WOULD OCCUPY quite a bit of Gaines's time going forward. Especially after he worked on Stevie Ray Vaughan's album, other blues artists and their record labels quickly came calling. "My phone was just about ringing off the wall. My life went from being a rock guy to being a blues guy," Gaines said. "I was even approached by one of the major record companies to start my own label. It never happened, but I had couple of meetings in New York to discuss the possibility."

George Thorogood ("Bad to the Bone") was one of the artists who approached Gaines. "We had a meeting in New Orleans, and his manager asked me if I would be interested in working with him," Gaines relates. "He wanted to do a record just with George alone, accompanied only by a metronome, and then afterwards we'd overdub the band. I said, 'No way. He's a rocker and he *needs* to record with his band.' Nevertheless, they went to LA and tried their approach, but I didn't think it worked. Sure enough, they called me again for the next album and agreed to record with the band. George and I ended up doing four records together over the years, and we're planning to maybe do another in the near future. We have a great relationship and I love working with everyone in his organization. He's a true rock and roller as well as a blues man. I ended up getting some songs on his gold record *Greatest Hits: 30 Years of Rock*. Yes, I love working with George Thorogood."

Gaines also got a call from actor Steven Seagal's management, asking him to come to LA and audition. "I said, 'I don't do auditions,' and I passed," Gaines remarks.

"David Lee Roth came into town for a couple of days to meet and talk to me about doing a blues album with him. He played me his songs, but they all sounded like show tunes. I asked him, 'Where's the blues material?' Then he told me about the last project he had done. He took six weeks off in the middle of it to go to New Guinea and walk across the country. So I asked him, 'What the heck am I going to do while you take that kind of time off?' I passed on that one, too."

Gaines has many stories connected with Coco Montoya, the blues guitarist who performed with such greats as Albert Collins and John Mayall. "I recorded his first three solo albums. One time, we were recording at Beale Street Studio. He had been struggling with getting his vocals together. In fact, it was kind of weird: he seemed to will himself to become sick when it came time to do the vocals, almost like a psychosomatic thing. He was reading *Mix* magazine, and he came across an article about haunted recording studios that mentioned the place we were working in. He said to me, 'Gaines, you know this place is haunted.' I said I knew it was, but fortunately, it was haunted by friendly ghosts.

"Well, the next day, he walked in and swore to me that he saw one. I just laughed it off. That night he was singing in the studio with the lights turned down low, and he was struggling again, so I said, 'Coco, who is that standing behind you?' The headphones went flying, the music stand went down, and he came flying into the control room. He then lifted me up by my shirt and said, 'Man, I almost had a heart attack from you telling me that.' But you know what? The next day we got all the vocals done and got out of there."

Gaines also ended up doing one more album with Huey Lewis and the News. The sessions took place in Memphis. Ironically, Gaines and the band had barely spoken in many years. The album would be called *Soulsville.*

"Bob Brown, Huey's manager, wanted to put us together one more time," Gaines explains. "We did it at Ardent and made it as live sounding as we could. We had fun doing it and it rekindled our relationship. We still stay in touch with each other. Huey has lost a lot of his hearing due to an incurable ear condition, but I do try to check on him. He also came to see us when Sandy and I got our big brass notes on the sidewalk on Beale Street, and he gave a little speech on our behalf. I'm grateful to Huey for that."

Then there were the Radiators, a band that has long been considered one of the foremost music ambassadors for New Orleans. "They're huge down there," Gaines insists. "We started the recording at Trent Reznor's studio in New Orleans, which is actually an old mortuary. The studio itself is where the bodies were prepared for burial, which was kind of creepy to think about. I stayed in one of the rooms upstairs where the drivers who would retrieve the bodies lived. It was decorated all in dark purple and other similar tones. The lighting was turned very low as well. I have recorded in some interesting places, but nothing like this. It was very spooky. I loved working with the band, but I have to admit I was glad to get out of there."

Gaines initially recorded an album with Walter Trout for a Dutch label that was released only in Europe. At the time, he had nothing happening in the United States. When they were finished with the recording, Gaines introduced Trout to Thomas Ruf of the German Ruf Records label, and he ended up signing with him.

"I recorded three of his records after that," Gaines recalls. "Walter is a great songwriter, a terrific guitar player, and a very emotional singer. He went through some severe medical problems but has since recovered, and now he's doing well. We always had a great time doing his records, and I still love his family."

Gaines had recorded Joanna Connor in the United States prior to recording a live album at the famous Frannz club in East Berlin, a year after the Berlin Wall came down. "We brought in a mobile truck from Sweden and spent two nights there. The first hotel they put us in looked like something out of a 1930s movie. There was one bathroom for the entire floor, and the overhead light was attached to a single wire that hung from the ceiling. I told them that we had to change hotels. So the next hotel they put us in was the old KGB headquarters. That inspired me to go around talking into the lampshade and the odd furniture pieces to see if anyone might be listening."

On the second day there, Gaines brought the rhythm guitar player into the remote truck to fix some parts. "As he was playing, he collapsed right into my arms. I laid him down and noticed there was blood on the back of his pants. We called the ambulance and got him to the hospital. He had torn his colon somehow, and we ended up having to leave him there for a couple of weeks."

Gaines also points proudly to the three albums he recorded with blues guitarist Jimmy Thackery. "Here again, there are lots of stories, but one of my favorites is about the time Jimmy invited a rather famous piano player named Jimmy McCracklin to come and guest on one of his songs. McCracklin was set up in the studio with his back to me. As we were tracking the song, he started out by playing in the wrong key. As he was playing away, Thackery was looking at me and mouthing to me, 'Who's gonna tell him?' After finishing the song, I brought them all into the control room and played back the song. Then I stopped it in the middle and said to him, 'Mr. McCracklin, I think you're in the wrong key.' He listened, looked at me, and said, 'Gaines, you've got the best ears in the world, and you're right.' Thackery looked at me and simply said 'Thank you.'"

Gaines also did three records with another great bluesman, Tommy Castro, and later recorded four albums with his wife, Sandy Carroll, as well as working on recordings by Lonnie Brooks, Kay Kay and the Rays, Buddy Miles and Rocky Athas, Dave Hole, Michael Burke, James Solberg, Devon Allman, a pair with the blues supergroup Royal Southern Brotherhood, three with Bernard Allison, three with Albert Cummings, and three with Joanne Shaw Taylor.

"There are many more blues project that I've done that aren't even listed," Gaines insists, noting that his upcoming blues efforts include Big Daddy Wilson, Doug MacLeod, Zac Harmon, Ally Venable, and Wee Willie Walker.

"They're all great," Gaines adds. "I've been blessed to have a great career and to have worked with so many talented people.

000

There's one date that Gaines, as well as most Americans who were alive at the time, can never forget: 9-11-2001. "I was at Willie Nelson's studio outside of Austin, Texas," he remembers. "I was working with Los Lonely Boys, doing demos for them to shop to the labels. Of course, this was before their big hit 'Heaven.'

"We had been working there about a week, when one morning my wife, Sandy, called me and told me to turn on the television. I watched as the first of the Twin Towers was burning, and then as the second plane was hitting the other tower. I couldn't believe it. I called the band's hotel room and told them to turn on their TV. Then I went to their room and said to them, 'Boys, the world has changed this morning, and it will never be the same after what has happened right now.'

"Naturally, I wanted to get home as soon as I could, but all the flights across the US had been grounded. Several days later, after flights began again, I drove to the airport. Unfortunately, I couldn't get into the rental car section because it was blocked off. As a result, I had to leave my car on the road that led into the airport. When I went inside, I saw that there were a lot of police officers and National Guard troops toting heavy-duty firearms. I went through at least three checkpoints where I had to show my ID. When I got on the plane, there were only two other people on the flight.

"When people ask what I remember most about that terrible day, that's the experience that I share."

CHAPTER 43

And Here We Are Today

WITH ALL THE STORIES GAINES has to share, there are still many left to tell. He says that those will perhaps have to wait for another time. "There have been so many artists that I would have liked to mention and to share stories about, but it would take another book to fit them all in," he says.

As this book was being written, in April 2020, the coronavirus was taking its toll and putting life on hold. "I've had to cancel three months' worth of projects due to the virus," Gaines says. "Three will likely be rescheduled for later this year, and one will probably go away. It is possible that two more will be done this fall."

Gaines does most of his work these days from his home studio in Stanton-ville, Tennessee. "This is the house my wife, Sandy, grew up in. It was built in 1910 and given a few additions in the midfifties. Before Sandy's mom passed away, I had promised her I would try and hold on to their house as long as I could," Gaines reflects. "We call it 'Miss Bessie's Place' now.

"And by the way, for those who aren't aware of my wife, Sandy Carroll Gaines, she's a singer, piano player, and songwriter who started playing pro-fessionally at the tender age of fifteen," Gaines says. "She went to college on a piano scholarship and frequently toured with a show band in which she was the only woman. She was also one of the first female players on Beale Street after it was redeveloped, and she played there for a number of years. She has her own brass note in the sidewalk in recognition of her history there. My note is one over, with Al Green's between us and Sam and Dave right next to us. Not bad company."

The couple recently celebrated their twentieth anniversary. "I have to just say 'thank you' to Sandy for putting up with all the crazy times and travel the last twenty years," Gaines says. "She is a very talented artist herself, not to mention a beauty queen."

Up until a year after Sandy's mother passed, the property wasn't being used, so Gaines decided to install some gear there to create a small production studio where he could record for Sandy and also have a songwriting space. "We had started with the gear in my home office, but I have never intended it to be a working studio. I promised myself years ago that I would not own a studio. I've run major studios, and they always create problems."

Even though Gaines had set up the space just for personal use, word somehow reached Thomas Ruf that he had a place to possibly record a few projects. "He had just signed Joanne Shaw Taylor, and they both wanted me to do her record. Sure enough, she came over from England, and we recorded it here. The record did really well, and Thomas sent another artist from Austria to work with me, followed by one from Canada. So here I was, the owner of an instant international studio. I hadn't planned any of this, mainly because at the time, I was still traveling a lot with Santana as well as other artists. Then other people started calling, and it hasn't stopped since. It's been going on for over ten years. Ironically, I had only put a bare minimum amount of gear in here, because I thought I might stop working at any time."

Gaines still does some traveling to record in other places, although he'll normally bring the results back and mix them at his home studio. "It saves a lot of money, and I don't have to travel as much," he says. "Sandy loves it because I can be home at night while working. Still, I'm not sure how long I will keep the studio going. I'm hoping to keep it going as long as my health allows."

EPILOGUE

AS JIM GAINES SHARES his life story, he tells of experiences with people who left an indelible imprint on the trajectory of modern music over the course of half a century. Gaines himself can take credit for helping to make that music and for shaping the soundtrack for so many lives. And, as he shared near the beginning of this account, the trajectory of his life is all the more remarkable considering his humble origins.

Born in Wynne, Arkansas, in 1941, Gaines was raised on a cotton farm, where his father worked as a sharecropper. "We lived in a shotgun shack house that had two rooms," Gaines relates. "The front part was the farm owner's one-room grocery store, which was mainly for the people who lived and worked for him on the farm. The second room was where we lived. It had no running water—there was a hand pump located outside—and no bathroom other than an outhouse. The only heat we had was from a coal stove in our quarters. That's how a lot of poor country folks lived at the time. My mom and I would run the store while my dad was in the fields working.

"For those who don't know what a sharecropper is, it's a person or an entire family that works for a farmer. Sometimes a small, rundown house is supplied, but typically you're given a modest salary, and if you're lucky, a small parcel of land that you can use to raise your own crops and then share the profit with the owner."

Despite their exceedingly modest circumstances, the family had a good life, Gaines says. "We were relatively happy kids and we managed to have some fun, but we all had to work. The worst part of it was picking cotton. Dragging that sack down the rows on your knees or stooping down to pluck the cotton really took a physical toll. Chopping the cotton (to eliminate the weeds) was almost as bad. You'd be in the fields at daybreak, before it got too hot, because the summer heat could be grueling. There are no shade trees in the fields, just long rows of cotton and weeds that had to be chopped.

"On Saturday night, we would all go to town and maybe go see a movie that cost all of ten cents or maybe buy a new comic book that cost about the same amount. It was cheap entertainment, but for us it was still a luxury."

Gaines and his family moved to Memphis when he was in the fifth grade, and he lived and worked there until 1970, before moving to San Francisco. "Moving to the big city of Memphis was a major change in our life," he says. "That meant no more forty-minute bus rides to get to school, no fields to work, and the luxury of running water and a real bathroom. It was like a miracle. When I tell my grandkids, and even some of my adult friends, what we went through, they think I'm exaggerating. 'Who could live like that?' they ask me. The thing is, when you do live like that, you learn to appreciate what you have and become very thankful for all the things life has given you.

"I've had a great career and the chance to work with some amazing artists and wonderful studio professionals. I love them all. I've also had the privilege of training a lot of amazing engineers throughout my life. I consider all of them members of my family."